Mama Cooks
CALIF🍊RNIA
Style
New Twists on Jewish Classics

This cookbook supports the life-enhancing work
of the Jewish Home for the Aging of Los Angeles

The Jewish Home for the Aging of Los Angeles is the largest residential care
facility for the elderly in California and is a leading national center for
Alzheimer's disease, aging, geriatrics and long-term care research.
This cookbook supports the life-enhancing work of
the Jewish Home for the Aging of Los Angeles.

ISBN 0-9654802-0-8
Library of Congress Catalog Card Number: 96-80095

First Edition, First Printing – May, 1997

Printed in the USA by

WIMMER

The Wimmer Companies, Inc.

Memphis

Cookbook Staff

Publisher: Meyer Gottlieb
Cookbook Editor: Thelma Rifkind
Food Editor: Harriet Part, Home Economist

Associate Editor, Proof Reading: Claire Kunin
Director, Marketing & Sales: Irv White

Recipe Tasters and Testers

Barbara Bernstein
Katherine Cohen
Bobbi Delevie
Gloria Getzug
Anne Goldstein
Deena Gordon

Pattikay Gottlieb
Renay Gregg
Sandi Knoff
Harriet Part
Marsha Pink
Thelma Rifkind

Lillian Topin
Anita Tamar
Sherry Watnick
Monica Wolfe
Carol Zuckerman

Computer Processing

Deena Gordon
Gale Marsh

Susan Pleskus
Samantha Tansky

Proof Reading

Anne Goldstein
Harriet Part
Thelma Rifkind

Samantha Tansky
Sherry Watnick

Cookbook Layout and Cover Design

Eric Wechsler, grapherics

Cover

Photo, Creative Image, Gary Choppé
Food Stylist, Erin Walgamuth
Challah baked by Jess Rifkind

Marketing/Sales

Barbara Bernstein
Anne Goldstein
Pattikay Gottlieb
Harriet Markman

Linda Matloff
Diane Paletz
Harriet Part
Shana Passman

Susan Pleskus
Thelma Rifkind
Pearl Roseman
Zelda White

Project Coordinator: Michael Turner, Director of Public Relations, Jewish Home for the Aging

Sponsors

Our heartfelt thanks to our sponsors for their generous contributions.

Benefactors

LASHA (Los Angeles Sephardic Home for the Aging)

Patrons

The Guardians of the Jewish Home for the Aging
Irv and Zelda White Foundation

Contributors

Ruby and Mel Elliot

Sponsors

The Associates of the Jewish Home for the Aging
Carol and Marvin Baer
Janice and Sheldon Blumenthal
Rosanna and Arnold D. Bogart
Country Wide Home Loan, Inc.
Roberta and Harold Delevie
Sheila, Alvin and Steven Dick
Eleanore and Harold Foonberg
Anne and Denne Goldstein
The Ida Mayer Cummings Auxiliary of the Jewish Home for the Aging
Fern and Marvin Jubas
Sybil and Mannon Kaplan
John N. Levi, Jr.
Helen and Sam Longwill
Dorothy and Avram Salkin
Marcia and Richard Schulman
Valley Jewish Business Leaders Association
Gerrie Wormser

Introduction

Some of our most cherished childhood memories involve food. We remember gathering around the dining table for holiday feasts and special celebrations. Grandmother spent the day preparing favorite traditional dishes that were inspired by recipes from her mother and grandmothers. These rich and hearty dishes…chicken soup with matzo balls, kishka, strudel and blintzes…were often referred to as "comfort foods" which translates into higher calories, cholesterol, fat, sugar and salt.

A new generation of health-conscious diners are discovering updated versions of traditional Jewish dishes with a lighter touch, using the freshest ingredients and updated preparation techniques. *Mama Cooks California Style: New Twists on Jewish Classics* shows that eating healthy doesn't mean compromising on taste. Our tested, California-style recipes include a wide range of Old World favorites. Many are classic dishes synonymous with traditional Jewish cooking. Some recipes are old, some original, some gourmet, some "California-ized," but all have a splendid comfort food taste that will make your mouth water.

Recipes for *Mama Cooks California Style: New Twists on Jewish Classics* came from the residents, staff and friends of the Jewish Home for the Aging of Los Angeles. The Jewish Home was founded over 85 years ago and is the largest continuing residential-care facility for the elderly in California. Proceeds from the cookbook will be used to underwrite the life-enhancing activities for the residents (whose average age is 90) of the Jewish Home for the Aging. For those who wish a bit of nostalgia or are not as calorie conscious, be sure to turn to the last chapter, where you'll find recipes as they were prepared by your mother and grandmothers.

We hope you enjoy this delicious cuisine and rich heritage.

Table of Contents

Great Beginnings:

APPETIZERS & SOUPS

Lox and Cream Cheese Quesadilla

The idea for this recipe came from a well-known L.A. eatery — and it's wonderful.

> **4 flour tortillas, 10-inch diameter**
> **4 ounces whipped cream cheese**
> **6 ounces thinly sliced lox (smoked salmon)**
> **1 small red onion, thinly sliced, rings separated**
> **3 Roma tomatoes, cut into 12 slices**
> **2 teaspoons drained capers (optional)**
> **Butter and oil**
> **Sour cream for garnish**

Place the flour tortillas on a flat working surface. Spread a thin layer of whipped cream cheese on half of each tortilla. Divide lox evenly over cream cheese. Place onion rings and tomato slices over lox. Sprinkle each with about ½ teaspoon capers, if desired. Fold empty side of tortilla over filled half. Heat equal mixture of butter and oil (about ½ tablespoon) on large griddle. Cook two at a time on both sides until golden brown. Cut each tortilla into 4 wedges and serve with dollop of sour cream.

Makes 16 wedges.

Hint: Beat ½ of 8-ounce package "⅓ less fat" cream cheese with 1 to 2 tablespoons low-fat milk until creamy instead of "whipped cream cheese."

Caramelized Onion, Olive and Caper Cheese Bread Slices

An unusual combination of flavors that work!

- **2 large onions, cut into quarters**
- **2 tablespoons olive oil**
- **2 teaspoons sugar**
- **3 cups escarole leaves or spinach, torn into pieces**
- **¼ cup each golden and dark raisins**
- **½ cup Kalamata olives, pitted, halved**
- **1 tablespoon capers**
- **¼ cup pine nuts**
- **Salt and pepper to taste**
- **1 12-inch Italian flat round cheese bread**
- **2 cups shredded mozzarella cheese**

Cut onion quarters in half and separate sections. Sauté onions over moderate heat in olive oil until onions become tender. Stir in sugar; cook 5 minutes longer. Stir in escarole. When escarole has wilted, add raisins, olives, capers and pine nuts. Season to taste with salt and pepper. Remove from heat.

Place flat bread on cookie sheet. Sprinkle with grated cheese. Spoon onion mixture evenly over cheese. Bake in 350 degree oven for 15 minutes. Cut into wedges.

Makes 8 servings.

Deli-Style Whitefish Spread

This spread is similar to a popular appetizer served at your favorite deli.

> **8 ounces smoked whitefish, skin and bones removed**
> **2–3 tablespoons finely minced red onion**
> **4 ounces whipped cream cheese (may use light or fat-free)**
> **½ tablespoon snipped fresh dill**
> **Salt to taste**
> **Seasoned black pepper to taste**
> **Dash of liquid smoke**

In a mixing bowl, shred whitefish with a fork. Blend in remaining ingredients. Serve with buttered, toasted small bagel halves.

Makes approximately 1½ cups.

Smoked Salmon in Horseradish Cream

A very tasty way to stretch an expensive ingredient.

> **8 ounces smoked salmon, cut into small pieces**
> **½ cup finely minced green onions**
> **2 teaspoons fresh snipped dill**
> **¾ cup sour cream (may use light)**
> **2 tablespoons white horseradish**
> **1 tablespoon mayonnaise**
> **Salt and freshly ground pepper to taste**

Combine salmon, minced green onions and dill in mixing bowl. Add sour cream, horseradish and mayonnaise and blend. Season with salt and pepper. Serve with rye or pumpernickel crisps.

Makes 6 to 8 appetizer servings.

Deviled Lamb Riblets

Outstanding finger food!

1 ½ pounds meaty lamb riblets, trimmed of fat
Garlic salt to taste
Seasoned pepper to taste
4 tablespoons sweet-hot mustard
2 egg yolks
Fine dry bread crumbs
½ teaspoon thyme or dill or both
Non-stick vegetable spray

Season lamb riblets with garlic salt and pepper. Broil or grill until well browned and crispy. Drain on paper towels.

Combine mustard and egg yolks. Brush riblets on all sides with mustard paste. Season bread crumbs (you may use packaged seasoned bread crumbs) with thyme or dill. Dip mustard-coated ribs into seasoned bread crumbs. Place on broiler pan and spray lightly with non-stick vegetable spray. Place under broiler until browned on all sides.

Makes 4 servings (2 to 3 ribs per serving).

Hummus

Healthy and delicious!

> 1 (15-ounce) can garbanzo beans, drained
> 2 tablespoons tahini
> 2 cloves garlic, minced
> 1/3 cup fresh lemon juice
> Seasoned salt to taste
> Seasoned pepper to taste
> 1/4 teaspoon paprika
> Water as needed
> 2–3 teaspoons olive oil, if desired
> 1 tablespoon finely minced parsley

In bowl of food processor, put garbanzo beans, tahini, garlic, lemon juice, salt, pepper and paprika. Process until mixture is smooth. If hummus is too thick, add a tablespoon of water. Taste for seasonings. Turn into serving dish. Make a small indentation with back of spoon. Fill indentation with olive oil and sprinkle with minced parsley. Serve with pita crisps or sesame crackers.

Makes about 1¾ cups.

Smoked Salmon, Red Onion and Roma Tomato Bruschetta

A Jewish version of an Italian favorite.

> 12–16 garlic toasted sourdough baguette slices
> Whipped cream cheese
> 4 medium finely chopped Roma tomatoes
> 1 small thinly sliced red onion
> 3–4 ounces smoked salmon pieces

½ teaspoon dried dill (or 1½ teaspoons fresh)
Seasoned salt to taste
Garlic pepper to taste

Spread toasted bread slices very lightly with cream cheese. In a medium bowl, combine tomatoes, red onion slices, salmon pieces, dill and seasonings to taste. Divide salmon mixture between the 12 to 16 slices of bread.

Makes 4 to 6 servings.

Baba Ghanoosh (Eggplant Dip)

There are many names for this Middle Eastern specialty but Baba "Ghanoosh" has a nice ring to it.

1 large eggplant
Juice of 3 medium lemons
¼ cup bottled or canned tahini
2 cloves garlic, minced
2 tablespoons finely chopped parsley
1–2 teaspoons salt
½ teaspoon white pepper
Paprika

Put eggplant, which has been pierced with a knife in several places, on a cookie sheet. Bake in 450 degree oven, turning occasionally, for 50 to 60 minutes or until eggplant is soft to the touch. Put in plastic bag for 10 minutes. Remove from bag. Peel off skin. Cut eggplant into pieces. Put in bowl of food processor fitted with steel blade. Add lemon juice, tahini, garlic and 1 tablespoon of parsley; add salt and pepper. Puree until smooth. Put in serving bowl and sprinkle with remaining parsley and paprika. Serve with wedges of pita bread or crackers.

Makes 4 to 6 appetizer servings.

Smoked Salmon Tartare

Smoked salmon makes a great substitute for the raw meat usually found in "Tartare."

> 1/2 **pound smoked salmon, sliced**
> **2–3 tablespoons minced red onion**
> 1 1/2 **tablespoons tiny capers**
> **Minced fresh dill or dried dill to taste**
> **2 tablespoons finely minced parsley**
> **2 teaspoons fresh lemon juice**
> **2 tablespoons sour cream**
> **Dash liquid smoke (optional)**
> 1/2 **teaspoon garlic pepper**
> **Thin slices pumpernickel toast or crackers**

Place salmon slices together in a stack. Cut 1/4-inch strips in one direction; then cut 1/4-inch strips in the other direction so that you have 1/4-inch square pieces. In a large mixing bowl, combine salmon pieces and remaining ingredients, except for pumpernickel. Serve on toasted pumpernickel or crackers.

Makes enough for 16 appetizers.

Yogurt and Cucumber Dip
with Pita Chips

A light and tasty appetizer.

Dip

> ½ **pound hot house cucumbers, peeled**
> 1 **(8-ounce) container plain yogurt**
> 2 **teaspoons minced fresh dill**
> 1 **clove garlic, minced**
> ½ **tablespoon fresh lemon juice**
> ¼ **teaspoon seasoned salt, or to taste**
> **Fresh ground pepper to taste**

Pita Chips

> 4 **(6-inch) pita breads**
> 3 **tablespoons butter, melted (may use butter-flavored or olive oil spray)**
> **Sesame seeds**
> 2 **teaspoons dried thyme**
> 1 **teaspoon dried savory**
> **Garlic salt and pepper to taste**
> **Grated Parmesan cheese**

To Make Dip: Shred cucumbers with hand grater or in food processor with grater attachment. Drain in colander. In a large mixing bowl, combine grated cucumber with yogurt, dill, garlic, lemon juice, seasoned salt and pepper. Serve with pita chips.

To Make Pita Chips: Warm pitas in oven for a few minutes or in microwave for about 30 seconds on high, or until warm. Separate top of pitas from bottom. Brush inside of pitas with melted butter or spray until coated. Cut pitas into eighths to form triangles. Arrange triangles on 2 baking sheets.

In a small bowl, combine sesame seeds, thyme, savory, garlic salt and pepper. Sprinkle the mixture over the pitas. Top with a sprinkling of Parmesan cheese. Bake both pans in 350 degree oven for 8 minutes. Switch pans and continue baking until pitas are toasted, about 5 to 6 minutes longer.

Makes 2 cups and 64 pita chips.

Caviar Tart

This appetizer never fails to please – it's easy to put together and very good!

8 hard-cooked eggs
⅓ cup butter, melted, or mayonnaise
1 tablespoon grated onion
Garlic pepper to taste
1 pint sour cream (may use light)
1 (2-ounce) jar red or black caviar
Cucumber slices
Cocktail rye

Grate the eggs in a large mixing bowl. Add either melted butter or mayonnaise, onion and garlic pepper to taste. Stir until well combined. Press into 9-inch pie plate. Stir sour cream while in carton and then spread an even layer over eggs. Refrigerate 1 hour. Make a border around pie with caviar. Cover with plastic wrap and refrigerate until serving. Serve with cucumber slices and cocktail rye.

Makes 12 servings.

Gefilte Fish in a Lemon Box

You won't believe it until you try it!

1 (1½-pound) jar gefilte fish
1 (3-ounce) box lemon jello
1 (5-ounce) jar white horseradish

Remove broth from jar and bring to a boil. You should have 1¼ cups. If not, add boiling water. Dissolve gelatin in hot liquid and add horseradish. (Do not use red horseradish or creamy horseradish.) Set whole pieces of fish into a 5- to 6-cup mold or loaf pan and add the hot liquid mixture. Allow to set in refrigerator. Unmold onto a platter and garnish with parsley and olives or tomatoes.

Makes 6 to 8 servings.

Hint: You can also use small gefilte fish balls in place of regular size.

Mock Gefilte Fish

With this recipe, you can have "homemade gefilte fish" that will impress any "Balabusta" (an excellent and praiseworthy homemaker).

8 cups water
2 large onions, cut into chunks
2 large carrots, cut into chunks
2 stalks celery, cut into chunks
1 tablespoon salt
1 tablespoon chicken or vegetable bouillon mix
2 (6-ounce) cans solid white albacore tuna, drained
1 medium onion, chopped
1 medium carrot, chopped
⅔–1 cup matzo meal
1 egg
2 tablespoons finely minced parsley
1 teaspoon salt
Garlic pepper to taste
Sugar to taste

Put water into a 4½-quart stockpot. Add onions, carrots and celery. Stir in salt and bouillon mix. Bring to a boil and turn heat lower so stock just barely simmers. Cover pot while preparing fish.

In the bowl of food processor, put tuna, onion and carrot. Turn motor on and off in spurts until mixture is coarsely grated. Add matzo meal (start with ⅔ cup) and turn on and off until mixture is finely grated. Add more matzo meal if fish mixture looks too wet. Remove to a bowl. Stir in egg, parsley, salt, garlic pepper and approximately ½ teaspoon of sugar.

With wet hands, make fish balls the size of a large egg. Place carefully into simmering stock. Cover pot and cook for ½ hour. Uncover and cook for additional 30 to 40 minutes longer. Remove fish balls with slotted spoon. Place on flat dish. Cool and then cover. Refrigerate overnight before using.

Makes 10 to 12 pieces.

Vegetable Pizza Dip

This is a crowd pleaser that is easily put together.

I (8-ounce) package softened cream cheese (may use ⅓ less fat)
½ cup sour cream
I teaspoon oregano
⅛ teaspoon garlic powder (optional)
⅛ teaspoon crushed red pepper (optional)
½ cup pizza sauce
¼ cup chopped green pepper
¼ cup chopped onion
¼ cup chopped black olives
¼ cup chopped mushrooms
½ cup shredded mozzarella cheese

In a mixing bowl, beat together cream cheese, sour cream and desired spices. Spread evenly in a 9- or 10-inch quiche dish or pie plate. Spread pizza sauce over top. Sprinkle with chopped vegetables and bake in 350 degree oven for 10 minutes. Top with mozzarella cheese and bake an additional 5 minutes. Serve hot with pita chips, bagel chips or nacho chips.

Makes 6 to 8 appetizer servings.

Herring in a Hurry

An unusual combination of flavors in a "quick to put together" appetizer.

I (12-ounce) jar herring snacks in wine
I (4-ounce) jar pimientos, chopped
I small red onion, minced
I ¼ cups bottled chili sauce
2 tablespoons minced parsley
I tablespoon minced fresh dill or I teaspoon dried dill
Seasoned pepper to taste

Drain herring. Put in mixing bowl with pimientos, onion, chili sauce, parsley and dill. Add pepper to taste. Cover and marinate in refrigerator up to a week. Serve with cocktail rye.

Makes 6 servings.

Spinach Latkes with Caviar

Easily made ahead and refrigerated, these pancakes are great for a party.

2 (10-ounce) packages frozen chopped spinach, cooked, drained and squeezed dry
1 egg
¼ teaspoon seasoned salt
¼ teaspoon seasoned pepper
3 tablespoons heavy cream
8 ounces feta cheese, crumbled
Butter and olive oil for frying pancakes
Light or regular sour cream
1 (4-ounce) jar red caviar

In a medium-sized mixing bowl, combine spinach with egg, salt, pepper, cream and crumbled feta cheese. Heat a tablespoon each of butter and oil in griddle until butter sizzles. Form patties about 3 inches in diameter and ½ inch thick. Place on griddle. Repeat process, adding butter and oil as needed. Cook until browned on both sides. Serve warm with dollop of sour cream and a bit of caviar.

Makes 4 to 6 servings of 2 to 3 patties each.

"On the Fast Track"
Puree of Vegetable Soup

Super quick to prepare! Pureed vegetables make this soup creamy without adding cream.

1 tablespoon olive oil
1 small onion or leek, diced
1 clove garlic, minced
3 (10½-ounce) cans chicken or vegetable broth or homemade broth
2 medium potatoes, peeled and diced
1 (16-ounce) package frozen mixed vegetables
Salt and white pepper to taste
½ teaspoon chervil, if desired

Heat oil in a large 6-quart saucepan or Dutch oven. Add onions and stir until soft, but not brown. When onions begin to soften, add minced garlic and cook while stirring to make sure garlic doesn't brown, or it will become bitter. Add broth, diced potatoes and vegetables; bring to boil. Reduce heat and simmer about 25 to 30 minutes or until potatoes are soft. Remove from heat.

Puree soup in a food processor or blender. If using a hand blender, puree soup in the pot. Reheat before serving. Taste for seasonings and add salt and pepper to taste. Serve with croutons, if desired.

Makes 4 to 6 servings.

Hint: Can be doubled. Can be made ahead and frozen.

Stir-Fry Chili Chicken Soup

When the weather is cold, this soup will warm your heart – and toes too! If you have homemade chicken soup in the freezer, that would be great…but canned works just as well!

¼ **pound chicken tenders, cut into thin pieces**
1 tablespoon peanut oil
1½ cups thinly sliced carrots
1½ cups thinly sliced red and yellow peppers
1 medium onion, cut into thin, long slivers
3 stalks bok choy, chopped into small pieces
2 teaspoons chili powder (mild or hot) to taste
6 cups canned or homemade chicken broth
Fresh garlic and ginger to taste
2 tablespoons hoisin sauce
1–2 teaspoons chili paste with garlic
Sesame seed oil (optional)
Cooked rice or Chinese-style noodles (optional)

In a large 4-quart stockpot sauté chicken pieces in hot oil until chicken turns opaque. Add carrots, peppers, onions and bok choy. Stir-fry for 4 to 5 minutes. Stir in chili powder, broth, garlic, ginger, hoisin sauce, chili paste with garlic and sesame seed oil. Heat soup to boiling and then simmer for 10 minutes. Remove piece of ginger. Add rice or noodles and cook another 3 to 4 minutes until rice is heated or noodles are tender.

Makes 4 servings.

Spicy Tortilla Soup

This looks great on a buffet with garnishes displayed around serving bowl so guests can top their soup as they like.

6–8 corn tortillas (preferably blue corn for a colorful garnish)
1 tablespoon oil
3 cloves garlic, minced
1 medium yellow onion, finely chopped
4 large plum tomatoes, peeled and chopped
8 cups chicken or vegetable stock
1 tablespoon cumin
2 teaspoons chili powder
2 tablespoons fresh cilantro, chopped
2 bay leaves
Salt and pepper to taste
1 large ripe avocado, peeled and diced (prepare just prior to serving)
2 teaspoons fresh lemon juice
¾ cup cooked chicken breast, shredded
½ cup non-dairy sour cream substitute (optional)

Preheat oven to 350 degrees. Cut tortillas into thin strips. Place on ungreased baking sheet and toast in oven about 5 minutes, until crisp and lightly browned, watching closely. Remove from oven and reserve about 1 cup of tortilla strips.

In a large 4-quart stockpot, heat oil; add garlic and onions. Sauté over medium heat until lightly browned, stirring frequently. Stir in toasted tortilla strips (excluding 1 cup reserved strips), tomatoes, chicken or vegetable stock, cumin, chili powder, cilantro, bay leaves, and salt and pepper to taste. Reduce heat and simmer 40 minutes. Remove from heat and discard bay leaves. Cool soup for 15 minutes. Puree soup in blender or food processor. In a small bowl, toss avocado with lemon juice. Serve soup garnished with avocado, chicken and sour cream substitute (optional). Top with reserved tortilla strips.

Makes 8 servings.

Hint: Soup may be prepared one day ahead. Keep covered in refrigerator until ready to serve.

Cream of Pumpkin Soup

This soup is almost better than pumpkin pie.

1 leek, white part only, chopped
1 large onion, chopped
4 tablespoons butter or margarine
1 cup canned pumpkin puree
5 cups vegetable stock
1 bay leaf
1/2–1 teaspoon curry powder
1/4 teaspoon white pepper
1 teaspoon salt
1/4 teaspoon nutmeg
1 cup half-and-half or non-dairy substitute
Minced parsley
Salted pumpkin seeds, toasted (optional)

Sauté leeks and onions in butter or margarine until soft; cool slightly and puree in blender or food processor. Return to large 2½-quart saucepan. Add pumpkin, vegetable broth and seasonings. Simmer 15 minutes. Remove bay leaf. Add cream and heat through. Taste for salt. Serve with sprinkling of minced parsley and toasted, salted pumpkin seeds, if desired.

Makes 6 to 8 servings.

Cold and Creamy Cantaloupe Soup

Refreshing and flavorful! Women love this soup!

2 full cups cantaloupe pieces
3 tablespoons vanilla or lemon low-fat yogurt
2 tablespoons light sour cream
1–2 tablespoons sugar
Ground cinnamon to taste
1½ cups ice cubes

In a food processor bowl, using steel blade, or in a blender, puree cantaloupe, vanilla yogurt, sour cream, sugar and cinnamon with ice cubes until mixture is smooth and frosty. Do not make more than ½ hour before serving. Keep refrigerated until serving. May garnish with dollop of sour cream and sprinkling of cinnamon or sprig of fresh mint.

Makes 2 to 3 servings.

Quick Cold Beet Borscht

A refreshing and quick revival of an old summer favorite.

1 (¼-inch-thick) lemon slice, peel reserved
1¾ cups sour cream (may use light)
¼ teaspoon salt
Dash white pepper
⅓ cup chopped red onion
1 (8-ounce) can sliced beets, drained
1 cup crushed ice

Put all the ingredients, except for the ice, in food processor or in blender. Run motor for 20 to 30 seconds. Add ice and blend for another 30 seconds. If desired, garnish soup with dollops of sour cream.

Makes 3 to 4 servings.

Vegetable Stock

This is a flavorful base for many soups when you don't want to use chicken or beef stock.

2 medium brown onions, leave peel on for color, quartered
1–2 leeks, washed and sliced
4–5 large cloves garlic, peeled and halved
2–3 large carrots, cut into 2-inch pieces
2–3 stalks celery, cut into 2-inch pieces
2–3 parsnips, cut into 1-inch pieces
¼ cup chopped parsley
1 tablespoon salt
½ teaspoon pepper
1 bouquet garni
Salt and pepper to taste

Put all the ingredients in a 4-quart stockpot. Cover with water (about 4 to 5 cups) and bring to a boil over moderate heat. Lower heat so that soup will simmer. Partially cover for 1 hour. Remove lid and taste for salt and pepper. Strain. Stock can be refrigerated or frozen.

Makes about 1 quart.

Hint: To make your own fresh bouquet garni: Combine 3 sprigs fresh parsley, 1 sprig fresh thyme and 1 dried or fresh bay leaf, 1 sprig fresh marjoram and 1 sprig of fresh celery leaves. Dried version of the above can also be made and tied in a little cheesecloth bag.

White Gazpacho Soup

This soup can be prepared ahead, as well as the garnishes. It is a wonderful "pick-me-upper" when hot weather gets you down.

Soup

> 3 medium cucumbers, peeled, seeds removed
> 1 large garlic clove, minced
> 3 cups vegetable stock
> 2 cups light sour cream or nonfat plain yogurt
> 3 tablespoons white vinegar
> 1 tablespoon salt
> ½ teaspoon white pepper

Garnishes

> 3 medium tomatoes, chopped
> ½ cup finely minced parsley
> ½ cup sliced green onions
> ¾ cup toasted salted almonds
> ½ cup finely chopped red or yellow peppers

Cut cucumbers into chunks after seeds and soft centers have been removed. Place in bowl of food processor with garlic, half the stock, sour cream, vinegar, salt and pepper. Process until mixture is smooth and blended. Combine mixture in a large bowl with remaining stock. Cover and chill overnight. Serve soup in large bowl set in crushed ice and surrounded with bowls of the garnishes; or serve soup in bowls and let people spoon garnishes on top of soup.

Makes 6 servings.

Bread Basket:

BREADS, MUFFINS & SCONES

Banana Macadamia Nut Bread

Forget calories! This is pure heaven from heavenly Hawaii.

¾ cup sugar
½ cup butter or margarine
2 eggs
2 cups flour
1 teaspoon baking soda
½ teaspoon salt
1 tablespoon grated orange peel
1 cup mashed ripe bananas
¼ cup orange juice
1 teaspoon vanilla
1 cup flaked coconut
¾ cup coarsely chopped macadamia nuts (or walnuts)

In bowl of electric mixer, cream sugar and butter. Add eggs and blend. Combine flour, baking soda, salt and orange peel, and add to sugar mixture. Beat at low speed until well mixed. Add bananas, orange juice and vanilla. Continue beating until all the ingredients are thoroughly combined. Remove beaters from bowl. Stir in coconut and nuts. Batter will be thick.

Divide batter into 3 greased 5½" x 2" x 3" mini-loaf pans. Bake in preheated 350 degree oven for 25 to 35 minutes or until toothpick inserted in center comes out clean. (Batter can also be baked in a 9" x 5" x 3" loaf pan for 50 to 60 minutes.) Cool pans for 10 minutes before removing breads.

Makes 3 mini-loaves or 1 large loaf.

Bobbi's Banana Bonanza Bread

Moist and delicious!

3 large ripe bananas, peeled
1 cup sugar
1 egg
4 tablespoons butter, at room temperature
1½ cups flour
1 teaspoon salt
1 teaspoon baking soda
1 cup chopped walnuts (optional)
Grated peel of 1 medium orange

In bowl of electric mixer, blend bananas on slow speed until smooth. Add sugar and mix well on medium speed. Add egg and butter, and continue mixing. Add flour, salt and baking soda; mix until all is blended. Stir in walnuts and orange peel.

Pour batter into greased 9" x 5" x 3" loaf pan and bake in preheated 350 degree oven for 55 to 65 minutes, or until top is lightly browned and a toothpick inserted in center comes out clean. Remove pan and cool on rack.

Makes 1 large loaf.

Date Nut Bread

Dark and moist, this date nut loaf is very reminiscent of the one served years ago at the Van de Kamp Bakery, a famous Los Angeles landmark.

> 1 cup pitted dates, chopped
> 1 ½ teaspoons baking soda
> ¾ cup boiling water
> 2 eggs
> 2 teaspoons vanilla
> ¼ cup oil
> 1 cup sugar
> 1 ½ cups flour
> Dash salt
> 1 cup finely chopped walnuts

Combine dates, baking soda and boiling water. Let stand for 5 minutes. In a separate bowl, beat eggs; add vanilla and oil. Stir in sugar, flour and salt. Mix in nuts. Add date mixture and stir until blended. Do not overbeat.

Spoon batter into well-greased 9" x 5" x 3" loaf pan. Bake in preheated 350 degree oven for 65 to 75 minutes, or until toothpick inserted in center comes out clean. Cool for 10 minutes in pan. Loosen around edges and invert carefully on a rack to cool completely.

Makes 1 loaf.

Low-Fat Orange-Poppyseed Bread

This is an outstanding example of low-fat baking!

> **2 cups flour**
> **1 cup sugar**
> **1 teaspoon salt**
> **2 teaspoons baking powder**
> **2 tablespoons poppy seeds**
> **2 tablespoons butter or margarine, melted**
> **½ cup plus 2 tablespoons orange marmalade**
> **1 egg, beaten**
> **½ cup milk**
> **1 teaspoon grated orange peel**

In a mixing bowl, combine flour, sugar, salt, baking powder and poppy seeds. In another large bowl, stir the melted butter with ½ cup marmalade; add egg and mix well. Stir in milk and orange peel; blend well. Add the flour mixture and stir batter until just combined.

Spoon batter into greased 8½" x 4½" x 3" loaf pan. Bake in preheated 350 degree oven for 45 to 50 minutes. Brush top of loaf with remaining marmalade. Cool on rack for 10 minutes. Loosen edges and remove bread from pan. Serve warm.

Makes 1 loaf.

Pineapple Zucchini Bread with Pineapple Glaze

No matter how many times you serve this bread, it always receives raves!

Bread

> **2 cups flour**
> **2 teaspoons baking soda**
> **2 teaspoons cinnamon**
> **3 eggs**
> **½ cup vegetable oil**
> **¾ cup buttermilk**
> **2 cups sugar**
> **1 teaspoon vanilla**
> **2 packed cups shredded, peeled zucchini**
> **1 cup chopped walnuts**
> **½ cup golden raisins (optional)**
> **⅓ cup well-drained crushed pineapple (save juice for glaze)**

Pineapple Glaze

> **½ (3-ounce) package cream cheese**
> **2 cups powdered sugar**
> **Drained pineapple juice**
> **Milk**

To Make Bread: Combine flour, baking soda and cinnamon in a 4-cup mixing cup with lip for pouring. In bowl of electric mixer, mix eggs, oil, buttermilk, sugar and vanilla. Beat on low. Slowly add dry ingredients. Beat until mixture is blended. Stir in by hand the zucchini, walnuts, raisins and pineapple.

Grease two 8" x 4" x 2½" loaf pans; then line with wax paper to fit bottom of pans and grease again with vegetable shortening or unsalted butter or margarine. Spoon in batter. Bake in preheated 350 degree oven for 45 to 50 minutes or until tops spring back when touched. Cool in pans for 15 minutes. Loosen edges and invert on racks or flat plates. Pull off wax paper. Cool breads completely before adding Pineapple Glaze.

To Make Pineapple Glaze: Combine cream cheese with powdered sugar in bowl of electric mixer or food processor. Add drained pineapple juice and just enough milk so that glaze can be spread over tops of bread.

Makes 2 loaves.

Apple Upside-Down Cornbread

This is a great way to dress up a mix.

> 1 tablespoon butter or margarine
> 3 tablespoons pure maple syrup
> 1 tablespoon brown sugar
> ½ teaspoon cinnamon
> 2 large Pippin apples
> Lemon juice
> 2 (8½-ounce) boxes cornbread mix
> ½ cup milk
> 4 tablespoons maple syrup
> 2 eggs
> 1 teaspoon maple flavoring

In a large, heavy skillet, melt butter over medium heat. Add maple syrup, brown sugar and cinnamon; blend. Cook for 1 to 2 minutes to thicken.

Peel and core apples and slice into ¼-inch-thick slices. Squeeze lemon over apples. Add to pan and sauté until slightly softened, 5 to 8 minutes or until syrup is thick.

Remove pan from heat. Spoon mixture into bottom of a 9-inch square baking dish. Arrange apple slices in a pattern of circles or lines.

In a mixing bowl, combine cornbread mix, milk, syrup, eggs and flavoring. Beat just until combined; do not overbeat. Spread batter gently over apples. Bake in preheated 375 degree oven for 20 to 25 minutes. Cool in pan for 5 minutes. Loosen edges and invert on serving plate.

Makes 9 servings.

Buttery Herb Bread

Years ago, Chef Mike Roy called me for this recipe while he was broadcasting his show on KNX radio. He knew a good thing when he heard it. **Harriet Part**

> 1 (1-pound) unsliced Sourdough or Sheepherders' bread
> 1 cup soft butter or margarine
> 1/3 cup finely minced parsley and chives
> 1/2 teaspoon dried savory
> 1/2 teaspoon dried thyme
> 1/2 teaspoon garlic salt
> 1/4 teaspoon seasoned black pepper
> Sesame seeds or poppy seeds (optional)
> Parmesan cheese

With sharp serrated knife, cut bread diagonally into 2-inch crosswise slices, about 2 inches from bottom crust. Then cut diagonally in opposite direction to form diamonds.

In bowl of food processor, using steel blade, combine butter, parsley, chives, savory, thyme, garlic salt and pepper and seeds. Spread over cut bread surfaces, top and sides. The bread can be wrapped and refrigerated or frozen at this point.

When ready to bake, bring bread to room temperature. Sprinkle with grated Parmesan cheese. Wrap in foil. Bake on cookie sheet in preheated 400 degree oven for 18 minutes. Open foil and continue baking for 6 minutes until golden.

Makes 8 servings.

Chunky Apple Streusel Muffins

Great muffins for a brunch!

Streusel Topping
> ¼ cup brown sugar
> 2 tablespoons flour
> Dash cinnamon
> 1 tablespoon melted butter

Muffins
> ¾ cup sugar
> ¼ cup oil
> ½ cup low-fat buttermilk
> 1 large egg
> 2 large egg whites
> 2 teaspoons vanilla
> 1½ cups flour
> 2 teaspoons baking powder
> ½ teaspoon baking soda
> 1 teaspoon cinnamon or apple spice
> 2 medium apples, cut into small chunks (about 2 cups)

To Make Streusel Topping: In a small bowl, toss together all streusel topping ingredients until small crumbs are formed. Refrigerate until ready to use.

To Make Muffins: In bowl of electric mixer, combine sugar and oil until smooth. Add buttermilk, egg, egg whites, and vanilla; blend into sugar mixture. Add 1 cup flour, baking powder, baking soda and cinnamon to mixture. Blend but do not overbeat.

Toss apples with remaining ½ cup flour in a small bowl. By hand, stir apples into batter. Spoon into 15 lined muffin tins, about ⅔ full. Sprinkle Streusel Topping on each muffin. Bake in preheated 375 degree oven until golden brown, about 20 to 25 minutes or until toothpick inserted in center of muffin comes out clean.

Makes 15 muffins.

Hint: If you do not have low-fat buttermilk, combine ½ cup low-fat milk with 1½ teaspoons white vinegar.

Mini-Chocolate Cheese-Filled Muffins

These are so good, you can serve them as quick mini-cupcakes!

> 1 (3-ounce) package cream cheese (may use ⅓ less fat)
> 2 tablespoons sugar
> ½ cup walnuts (optional)
> 1 cup flour
> ½ cup sugar
> 3 tablespoons unsweetened cocoa
> 2 teaspoons baking powder
> ½ teaspoon salt
> 1 egg, beaten
> ¾ cup milk
> ⅓ cup oil
> Powdered sugar (optional)

In a small bowl, blend cream cheese and 2 tablespoons sugar until fluffy. Stir in chopped walnuts, if desired. Set aside.

In a large bowl, stir flour, sugar, cocoa, baking powder and salt. Make well in center of dry ingredients. Combine egg, milk and oil. Add all at once to dry ingredients, stirring until moistened. Batter should be lumpy.

Spoon about 1 tablespoon chocolate batter into each cup of 12-cup mini-muffin pan. Drop 1 teaspoon cream cheese mixture on top of each and then more chocolate batter. Bake in preheated 375 degree oven for 20 minutes. Dust with powdered sugar, if desired.

Makes 12 muffins.

Nonfat Apple Bran Muffins

Moist, delicious and nonfat!

Muffins

> 1 cup whole wheat flour
> 3 teaspoons baking powder
> ½ teaspoon salt
> 1 cup bran flakes, finely crushed
> 2 egg whites
> 3 tablespoons molasses
> 3 tablespoons applesauce
> 1 cup nonfat milk

Optional (use any one of the following)

> 1 cup raisins
> ½ cup canned pineapple tidbits, squeezed dry
> 1 cup currants
> 1 cup date pieces

In a medium bowl, mix flour, baking powder and salt with bran flakes; then set aside. Beat egg whites in another bowl; add molasses, applesauce and milk. Add dry ingredients and mix only enough to moisten flour. Add optional ingredient at this time.

Fill paper muffin cups in muffin pan. Bake in preheated 400 degree oven for 15 minutes.

Makes 12 muffins.

Fat-Free Berry Oatmeal Muffins

Chewy and tasty – and very easy to make. Applesauce takes the place of fat and adds a delicious flavor.

> 1 cup fresh or frozen berries (blueberries, raspberries or cranberries)
> 1 tablespoon flour
> 1½ cups flour
> 2 teaspoons baking soda
> ⅔ cup nonfat milk
> ¾ cup oatmeal
> ½ cup sugar
> ½ cup applesauce
> 1 egg white (or ¼ cup egg substitute)

Toss berries with 1 tablespoon flour. Set aside. Mix remaining ingredients and fold in the floured berries. To avoid doughy muffins, try not to overbeat.

Pour batter into oil-sprayed muffin cup pan. Bake in preheated 400 degree oven for 20 to 25 minutes.

Makes 1 dozen muffins.

Fat-Free Pumpkin Bread or Muffins

"I teach this bread to my cooking classes and they love it. You can also make muffins with the same recipe." **Nancy Fox**

> 3 egg whites
> 1 cup sugar
> ½ cup minus 1 tablespoon unsweetened applesauce
> 1 cup canned pumpkin
> 1 cup flour
> 1 teaspoon baking powder
> ½ teaspoon baking soda
> ½ teaspoon salt
> 1 teaspoon cinnamon
> ½ teaspoon pumpkin pie spice

Beat egg whites with hand mixer until foamy. Add sugar, applesauce and pumpkin. Mix until blended. Add remaining ingredients. Mix until thoroughly combined.

Prepare an 8" x 4" x 3" loaf pan or two mini-muffin pans with non-stick spray. Pour batter into prepared pans. Bake in preheated 350 degree oven for approximately 1 hour or until toothpick comes out clean.

Makes 1 loaf (12 slices) or 24 mini-muffins.

Hint: *When making muffins, bake for only 15 to 20 minutes.*

Cherry-Nut Whole Wheat Scones

Wonderful to serve at a tea.

2 cups whole wheat flour
2½ teaspoons baking powder
½ teaspoon salt
½ cup sugar
1 stick cold butter, cut into pieces
1 extra-large egg
½ cup milk
½ cup dried cherries, strawberries or blueberries
½ cup chopped pecans
2 tablespoons milk (for wash)

In a mixing bowl, combine flour, baking powder, salt and sugar. Using fingertips, work in butter until mixture is crumbly. In another bowl, beat egg and milk. Make a well in center of the flour mixture and add egg mixture, cherries and nuts. Stir with a fork until dough forms. Knead in bowl 5 to 8 times until smooth.

Turn dough out on lightly floured board. Knead 2 to 3 times more. Pat dough into a ¾-inch-thick circle. Carefully put circle on foil-lined baking sheet. Using a sharp knife, score (without slicing all the way through) into 12 equal wedges. Brush with milk. Bake in preheated 425 degree oven for 15 to 18 minutes or until lightly browned.

Makes 12 scones.

Butter Scones
with Orange Cheese Spread

Preserved ginger is an exciting addition to these scones.

Scones

> **2 cups sifted flour**
> **¼ cup sugar**
> **2 tablespoons baking powder**
> **6 tablespoons cold butter, cut into pieces**
> **⅔ cup milk**
> **1 egg, beaten**

Orange Cheese Spread

> **1 (8-ounce) package softened cream cheese (may use ⅓ less fat)**
> **¼ cup powdered sugar**
> **2 tablespoons milk**
> **2 tablespoons frozen orange juice concentrate**
> **Dash nutmeg**

To Make Scones: Sift flour, sugar and baking powder in bowl. Add butter and blend with fingers until mixture resembles coarse meal. Stir in milk until blended. Dough will be sticky. Turn out on floured board and knead. Roll into a rectangle about ½ inch thick. With sharp knife, cut into diamond shapes.

Place dough on lightly greased baking sheet. Brush with beaten egg. Bake in preheated 350 degree oven for 15 minutes. Serve with Orange Cheese Spread.

To Make Orange Cheese Spread: Combine all ingredients for Orange Cheese Spread in bowl of electric mixer; beat until blended and serve with scones.

Makes 8 to 10 servings.

Hint: Add preserved ginger, cut into small slices, to the batter for a wonderful flavor.

Poppyseed Toast

Quick, easy and very good!

> **12 thin slices white bread**
> **Butter**
> **Poppy seeds**

Trim crusts from white bread and flatten each slice with a rolling pin. Spread the slices with butter and sprinkle with poppy seeds. Roll up the slices, secure them with toothpicks, and arrange them on a buttered baking sheet. Brush with melted butter and sprinkle with more poppy seeds. Bake in preheated 425 degree oven for 10 minutes or until golden brown. Remove picks and serve at once.

Makes approximately 12 servings.

Onion Pockets

This is a bakery favorite that you can easily make at home. The aroma is wonderful and so is the roll.

> **1 (13¾-ounce) package hot roll mix**
> **2 cups finely chopped onions**
> **½ cup butter**
> **Salt and pepper to taste**
> **Poppy seeds**

Prepare dough according to package directions. While dough is rising for first time, prepare filling. Sauté onions in butter until golden but not browned. Season with salt and pepper (garlic may be added, if desired) and cool. After kneading dough for 2 minutes, roll dough to ¼ inch thickness and cut into rectangles 3" x 4". Put a scant teaspoon of onion in center. Fold ⅓ of dough over filling; then add a scant teaspoon of onion and fold over again.

Put pockets on cookie sheets about 3 inches apart and let rise in warm place for 30 to 40 minutes or until doubled. Brush with any remaining butter-onion mixture. Sprinkle with poppy seeds. Bake in preheated 350 degree oven for 12 to 15 minutes or until golden.

Makes approximately 12 pockets.

Matzo Bagels (Passover)

This proves anything is possible if you want it badly enough!

    1⅓ cups water
    ⅔ cup oil
    2 tablespoons sugar
    1 teaspoon salt
    2 cups matzo meal
    6 eggs

Combine water, oil, sugar and salt in a 1½-quart saucepan. Bring to a boil and stir in matzo meal. Remove from heat and cool. Beat in eggs, one at a time. Chill.

With greased hands, roll dough into 2-inch balls. Place on 2 greased cookie sheets. Make deep indentations in center of each ball with wet finger. Bake in preheated 350 degree oven for 40 minutes. Reduce heat to 300 degrees and bake for 15 minutes more.

Makes about 18 matzo bagels.

Hint: Bagels can be used instead of bread for sandwiches — they are also wonderful toasted.

Greens, Fresh and Fancy:

SALADS, DRESSINGS & RELISHES

Marinated Harvest Salad

Easily put together – perfect for a party!

6 zucchini, parboiled for 3 to 4 minutes
1 medium red onion, sliced
1 medium green pepper, sliced
1 medium red pepper, sliced
1 box cherry tomatoes
1 (16-ounce) can sliced black olives, drained
¼ cup finely chopped parsley
1 (14-ounce) can garbanzo beans, drained
⅓ cup wine vinegar
⅔ cup oil
1 teaspoon Italian seasonings (oregano, basil and thyme)
1 tablespoon capers
¼ teaspoon mustard
2 cloves garlic, minced
Salt and pepper to taste

After parboiling zucchini, drain and refrigerate until cold. Slice zucchini into thin diagonal slices. Put in large bowl and add remaining ingredients. Season well and refrigerate for 2 to 3 hours.

Makes 6 servings.

Hint: Can be made at least 2 days ahead.

California Mediterranean Salad

Armenians call it Armenian salad; Israelis call it Israeli salad. We just say, "It's a great salad!"

    3 ripe tomatoes, diced
    I large cucumber, peeled, cut into chunks
    I small red onion, finely minced
    2 small avocados, peeled, pitted and cubed
    ¼ cup minced parsley
    ¼ cup fresh lemon juice
    2 tablespoons olive oil
    Salt and black pepper to taste
    ½ cup Kalamata olives

Combine diced tomatoes, cucumbers, minced onion, cubed avocados and parsley. Whisk together lemon juice and olive oil and pour over salad. Season with salt and pepper to taste. Toss with olives and serve.

Makes 4 servings.

Mama's California Bow-Tie Pasta Salad

This salad looks beautiful when served in hollowed-out large tomatoes.

    I (8-ounce) package bow-tie pasta
    ½–⅔ cup sun-dried tomatoes, drained from oil and finely chopped
    ⅓ cup fresh basil, minced
    ⅓ cup pitted Kalamata olives, chopped
    ¾ cup feta cheese, crumbled
    2 tablespoons olive oil
    I½ tablespoons red wine vinegar
    Salt and pepper to taste

Cook pasta according to package directions. Drain. Cool to room temperature. In a large mixing bowl, combine pasta with remaining ingredients. Chill until serving time.

Makes 4 servings.

Spinach Salad with Pine Nut Dressing

The dressing "makes" this salad!

    ⅔ cup pine nuts
    7 tablespoons olive or salad oil
    2½ tablespoons wine vinegar
    ⅛ teaspoon ground nutmeg
    1 teaspoon salt
    ¼ teaspoon pepper
    ½ teaspoon grated lemon peel
    ½ teaspoon crumbled dry tarragon
    1½ pounds spinach leaves, washed well

Spread pine nuts in single layer in an 8- or 9-inch pie pan. Toast in 350 degree oven, stirring occasionally until golden, 5 to 8 minutes. Let cool. In a bowl, mix nuts with oil, vinegar, nutmeg, salt, pepper, lemon peel and tarragon. Cover and let stand at room temperature for at least 30 minutes, or as long as overnight.

Line 8 individual salad plates with large spinach leaves. Thinly sliver the remaining leaves and mound onto plates. Stir dressing to blend. Spoon equal portion over each salad. Serve at once.

Makes 8 servings.

Grilled Vegetable Salad with Goat Cheese

Grilled vegetables – the new "in" ingredient for salads.

Salad

      1 large yellow pepper, seeded and quartered
      1 large red bell pepper, seeded and quartered
      1 large green bell pepper, seeded and quartered
      4 slices eggplant (cut lengthwise)
      1 (7-inch) zucchini, cut diagonally into ¼-inch-thick slices
      Cooking oil (optional)
      Salt and pepper
      6–8 cups torn pieces Romaine lettuce
      4 ounces goat cheese, cut into pieces or slices

Mustard Wine Vinaigrette

      2 tablespoons red wine vinegar
      1 tablespoon balsamic vinegar
      1 tablespoon water
      1 tablespoon Dijon mustard
      ½ teaspoon garlic salt
      Dash white pepper
      ⅓–½ cup olive oil

To Make Salad: Grill peppers, eggplant and zucchini over hot coals until charred (but not burned) and tender. Brush or spray vegetables with oil during cooking, if desired. Season lightly with salt and pepper.

In a large salad bowl, combine grilled cut-up peppers, cut-up eggplant slices and zucchini slices. Mix in lettuce and toss with enough Mustard Wine Vinaigrette to moisten. Divide among 4 serving plates and garnish with goat cheese.

To Make Vinaigrette: Combine vinegars, water, mustard, garlic salt and white pepper. Whisk in oil.

Makes 4 servings.

Red and Green Pepper Salad

If you're serving a Mexican meal, this is a perfect accompaniment.

4 cups very finely diced celery
2 green peppers, seeded and finely diced
1 red pepper, seeded and finely diced
1 large red onion, finely diced
½ cup sliced pimiento-stuffed olives
2 teaspoons salt
1 teaspoon seasoned black pepper
1 tablespoon Dijon mustard
2 tablespoons red wine vinegar
6 tablespoons oil
2 tablespoons minced parsley or cilantro

Combine vegetables in a serving bowl. Mix salt, pepper, mustard, vinegar and oil, and pour over vegetables. Sprinkle with parsley or cilantro and toss. Prepare ahead and marinate in refrigerator for at least 3 hours.

Makes 6 to 8 servings.

Marrakesh Carrot Salad

Different than the usual carrot salad, but delicious!

> **12 large carrots, diagonally sliced**
> **2 tablespoons minced cilantro**
> **½ teaspoon cumin**
> **1 teaspoon coriander**
> **1 tablespoon paprika**
> **½ teaspoon minced garlic**
> **1 tablespoon sugar**
> **1½ teaspoons salt**
> **Ground black pepper to taste**
> **⅓ cup white vinegar**
> **2 tablespoons lemon juice**
> **3 tablespoons olive or sesame oil**

Steam carrots until barely tender. Drain and cool. Mix remaining ingredients together and pour over carrots. Marinate for at least 3 hours or overnight. Serve in lettuce cups or green pepper cups.

Makes 6 to 8 servings.

Eggplant Tomato Vinaigrette

This recipe was developed by Henry Winkler's ("the Fonz") mother-in-law many years ago, and it's more in vogue today!

Eggplant

>2 medium eggplants, long and narrow
>Salt
>1 (7-ounce) jar roasted red peppers, drained
>1 large red onion
>¼ bunch parsley, minced
>4–5 large tomatoes, each cut into 4 to 5 slices

Vinaigrette

>¼ cup wine vinegar or juice of ½ fresh lemon
>⅓ cup oil
>½ teaspoon sugar
>1 teaspoon Dijon mustard
>2 cloves garlic, minced
>Ground pepper to taste
>1 tablespoon capers
>1 tube anchovy paste (optional)

Bake eggplants in 400 degree oven until they blister and are soft to the touch, but not mushy. Remove from oven. Place in plastic bag and close for 10 minutes to make job of peeling much easier. Peel and slice into ½-inch slices. Place eggplant in large glass dish. Salt and set aside for 30 minutes. Press off excess liquid with paper towels. Cut red peppers into strips. Cut onion into very thin slices and separate into rings.

On a large serving platter, arrange 8 to 10 tomato slices. Layer eggplant on tomato slices, then onion rings, parsley and red pepper strips. Repeat layering. Combine dressing ingredients and spoon over stacks of eggplant and tomatoes. Marinate overnight.

Makes 8 to 10 servings.

Bullock's Tea Room
Chinese Chicken Salad

First Bullock's Wilshire closed. Then the Tea Room closed. Then Bullock's closed. But the Chinese Chicken Salad will go on forever!

Salad

> 10–12 cups of bite-sized pieces iceberg lettuce
> 3 cups cooked chicken breasts, shredded
> 1⅓ cups shredded carrots
> 1⅓ cups fresh bean sprouts
> ¾ cup sliced water chestnuts, drained
> 1 cup slivered almonds
> ½ cup finely chopped green onions

Dressing

> 1 (8-ounce) jar honey mustard (or mix equal parts honey and mustard)
> 4 tablespoons honey
> ¼ cup mayonnaise (may use light)
> ¼ cup non-dairy creamer
> ¼ cup red wine vinegar
> ¼ cup vegetable oil

Egg Roll Strips

> 1 (24-ounce) package, egg roll skins
> Oil for frying

To Make Salad: In a large mixing bowl, place lettuce and shredded chicken. Add carrots, sprouts, water chestnuts, almonds and chopped green onions. Refrigerate.

To Make Dressing: In a large mixing bowl, combine honey mustard, honey, mayonnaise and creamer with wine vinegar. Whisk in oil until blended. When ready to serve salad, mix in desired amount of dressing and toss. Sprinkle with Egg Roll Strips.

To Make Egg Roll Strips: Cut egg roll wrappers (from a 24-ounce package of refrigerated egg roll skins) into strips as needed. Heat 3 inches of vegetable oil in medium saucepan or wok until very hot and add a handful of strips at a time to the oil. Cook until golden. Use slotted spoon to remove strips from oil. Drain on paper towels. Make 4 cups of strips.

Makes 4 to 6 servings.

Hoisin Chicken Salad

If you like Chinese chicken salad, you'll love this one!

Marinade

      ¼ cup hoisin sauce
      2 tablespoons ketchup
      2 cloves garlic, minced
      1½ tablespoons soy sauce
      2 tablespoons rice wine or sherry
      1 tablespoon sugar
      1 tablespoon minced green onion
      1½–2 pounds chicken tenders

Salad

      6 cups torn lettuce and romaine leaves
      ½ cup sliced celery
      1½ cups blanched snow peas
      ½ cup thinly sliced carrots
      2 tablespoons finely chopped green onion

Dressing

      ⅓ cup soy sauce
      3 tablespoons rice vinegar
      1½ teaspoons sugar
      2 tablespoons sesame oil
      2 tablespoons vegetable oil
      Pinch red pepper flakes (optional)

To Make Marinade: In a large bowl, combine hoisin sauce, ketchup, garlic, soy sauce, rice wine, sugar and green onion. Cut chicken tenders into bite-sized pieces. Add to bowl and mix thoroughly to coat. Marinate overnight. Remove chicken from marinade. Broil or grill, about 8 to 10 minutes or until cooked through. Combine cooked chicken with greens and vegetables. Toss with Dressing.

To Make Salad: Prepare and combine salad ingredients in a large mixing bowl. Cover with a paper towel and plastic wrap and refrigerate until serving time.

To Make Dressing: Combine soy sauce, rice vinegar and sugar, plus sesame and vegetable oils. Add pepper flakes if desired. Set aside.

Makes 4 to 6 servings.

Fresh Salmon Salad

This was from a "well-known" gourmet take-out – it's a lot cheaper to make it yourself!

2–2½ cups flaked, cooked salmon (1 pound uncooked)
2 tablespoons minced Italian parsley
2 tablespoons minced fresh dill
2–3 tablespoons finely chopped green onions
1 tablespoon capers
2 tablespoons fresh lemon juice
Salt and pepper to taste
¼ cup light sour cream
⅓ cup low-fat mayonnaise

Combine all ingredients in mixing bowl. Can use as a salad with asparagus, tomatoes and greens; as an appetizer surrounded by small pumpernickel bread slices, crackers, and/or cucumber slices; or as a sandwich filling.

Makes 1½ cups.

Cole Slaw with Peanuts

Peanuts "make" this cole slaw!

> 1 medium head green cabbage, shredded
> 1 small red cabbage, shredded
> ½ bunch green onions, thinly sliced
> 2–3 carrots, shredded
> 1 small green pepper, shredded
> ¾ cup salad oil
> 3 tablespoons vinegar
> 3 tablespoons lemon juice
> 1 teaspoon salt
> ½ teaspoon seasoned pepper
> ½ teaspoon dry mustard
> ½ teaspoon paprika
> ¼ teaspoon sugar
> ½ teaspoon celery seeds
> 1 teaspoon grated onion
> 1 clove garlic, minced
> ½ cup salted peanuts (or chili peanuts)

In a large serving bowl, toss together shredded cabbages, onions, carrots and green pepper. Keep in refrigerator until ready to serve. Make dressing by combining next 11 ingredients, from salad oil to garlic. Keep in a covered jar. Shake dressing well before mixing with slaw. Season with salt and pepper to taste and toss with peanuts.

Makes 8 to 10 servings.

Annie's Asian Pasta Salad

Marco Polo knew what he was doing! We just went a little further.

1 pound spaghetti or linguini, cooked al dente
¼ cup sesame oil
⅓ cup soy sauce (can use low-sodium soy)
2 tablespoons sugar
2½ tablespoons red wine vinegar
2 teaspoons salt
1 cup chopped cilantro or Italian parsley
2–3 small jalapeños, seeded and minced or 1 large seeded and diced red pepper
8–10 green onions, slivered
½ cup peas or 1 cup sliced mushrooms or ½ cup sliced water chestnuts (optional)
1½ cups dry roasted peanuts or chili-flavored peanuts

Put cooked spaghetti in colander and rinse with cold water. Drain well and put in a large mixing bowl. In another bowl, combine sesame oil, soy sauce, sugar, vinegar and salt. Whisk until sugar has dissolved. Set aside. To the spaghetti, add cilantro, jalapeños (or peppers), green onions and peas, mushrooms or water chestnuts, if desired. Toss with dressing. Sprinkle peanuts over salad before serving.

Makes 8 to 10 side dish servings or 6 main course servings.

Tabouli

This salad is not only healthy, it's very good!

½ cup fine bulgur (cracked wheat)
1½ cups hot water
3 cups minced parsley
½ cup finely chopped green onions
1 medium tomato, diced
1 teaspoon salt
½ teaspoon pepper
¼ teaspoon allspice
3 tablespoons olive oil
3 tablespoons lemon juice
Romaine lettuce leaves

Soak bulgur in hot water until water is absorbed. Add parsley, onions, tomato and toss to mix. Combine salt, pepper, allspice, oil and lemon juice; add to bulgur mixture. Toss again. Chill. Serve in individual portions on romaine lettuce leaves.

Makes 6 to 8 servings.

Kasha and Bow-Tie Green Bean Salad

If you happen to have leftover "Kasha Varnishkes" (which is unlikely), this is a wonderful way to use it up!

Salad

> 4 cups cooked "Kasha Varnishkes" (see *I Remember Mama* chapter)
> ½ pound green beans, cooked or 1 (10-ounce) box frozen green beans, cooked,
> drained, cut into ½-inch pieces
> ½ cup grated carrots
> ¼ cup thinly sliced green onions
> ⅓ cup finely chopped radishes
> 1 tablespoon minced fresh dill

Scallion Vinaigrette

> ⅓ cup thinly sliced scallions
> ⅓ cup rice vinegar
> 1 teaspoon sugar
> 1 clove garlic, minced
> Pinch cayenne pepper
> Salt to taste
> ½ cup oil

To Prepare Salad: In a large bowl, combine "Kasha Varnishkes," green beans, carrots, green onions, radishes and dill.

To Prepare Vinaigrette: In a blender or food processor, puree the scallions with the vinegar, sugar, garlic, pepper and salt to taste. Add the oil in a stream until dressing is blended. Drizzle the salad with the dressing and toss together. Serve at room temperature.

Makes 4 to 6 servings.

Apricot-Pine Nut Couscous Salad

Outstanding as well as unusual – you'll want to serve this at your next buffet.

½ cup dried apricots, cut into quarters
½ cup currants or raisins
1 (12-ounce) box couscous, prepared according to package directions
⅓–½ cup virgin olive oil
1 bunch green onions, coarsely chopped
2 teaspoons orange peel
½ cup fresh orange juice
½ cup finely minced Italian parsley
¼ cup minced cilantro (optional)
1½ tablespoons fresh lemon juice
Seasoned salt and seasoned pepper to taste
Dash cumin (optional)
½ cup toasted pine nuts

In a large mixing bowl, place apricots and currants or raisins. Add warm couscous. Stir the oil through the couscous. Add remaining ingredients, except for toasted pine nuts, and toss. Taste for salt, pepper and cumin. When ready to serve, sprinkle top of salad with toasted pine nuts. Can be served warm or cold.

Makes 8 servings.

Strawberry Pretzel Salad

Testers had their doubts about this recipe – but they all said "yes, yes, yes" after the tasting.

> 2½ cups miniature pretzels, crushed into small pieces (approximately ¼ inch)
> 5 tablespoons brown sugar
> ¾ cup margarine or butter, melted
> 1 (6-ounce) package strawberry gelatin dessert
> 2 cups boiling water
> ¼ cup ice water
> 1 (8-ounce) package cream cheese, at room temperature
> 1 cup sugar
> 1 (8-ounce) container non-dairy topping
> ½ cup ice water
> 2 (10-ounce) packages frozen strawberries, thawed

Preheat oven to 350 degrees. Spray bottom of 9" x 13" shallow baking dish with vegetable spray or grease with margarine or butter.

In a mixing bowl, combine crushed pretzels, brown sugar and melted butter, mixing well. Spoon into prepared baking dish and spread evenly over bottom, pressing lightly to make a crust. Bake in 350 degree oven for 10 minutes. Cool completely.

In a medium bowl, dissolve gelatin in 2 cups boiling water. Add ice water and stir. Chill until partially set, about 1 hour and 30 to 45 minutes.

In a large bowl, mix cream cheese, sugar, non-dairy topping and ½ cup ice water with fork until blended. Spread evenly over cooled pretzel crust. Refrigerate. When gelatin is partially set, stir in strawberries and pour entire mixture over cream cheese mixture. Cover and chill until set, at least 4 hours.

Makes 10 to 12 servings.

Variation: Can substitute peach gelatin dessert for strawberry gelatin and frozen peach slices instead of strawberries.

Thai Tomato Salsa for Fish

Men love this spicy, hot salsa!

2 scallions (leave 3 inches of green), slivered lengthwise
2½ tablespoons fresh lemon juice
1–1½ bunches cilantro (leaves removed), minced
2 cloves garlic, minced
4 ripe medium tomatoes, seeded and diced
4 tablespoons minced red onion
1½ teaspoons grated fresh ginger
1 tablespoon balsamic vinegar
½ cup olive oil
Salt and pepper to taste

Combine all ingredients in a bowl and allow to sit for at least ½ hour before serving. Can be served over grilled, broiled or roasted meats or fish. Also good with chips.

Makes 6 servings.

Honey Mustard Vinaigrette

A very popular dressing in all the "hot" restaurants!

¼ cup red wine vinegar
1 tablespoon fresh lemon juice
2–3 tablespoons honey
1 tablespoon Dijon mustard
½ teaspoon minced fresh garlic
1–2 teaspoons salt
¼–½ teaspoon ground pepper
¼–⅓ cup oil

In a small bowl, whisk together vinegar, lemon juice, honey, mustard, garlic, salt and pepper. Whisk in oil. Taste for salt and pepper, add if needed.

Makes approximately 1 cup.

Hint: *Great over vegetables or chicken salad.*

Ranch-Style Low-Calorie Dressing Mix

Great for dieters! Delicious as a salad dressing or a dip.

Dressing Mix

    1 cup powdered buttermilk
    1 ½ teaspoons seasoned salt
    1 ½ teaspoons garlic pepper
    1 tablespoon garlic powder
    2 ½ teaspoons onion powder
    3 tablespoons dried parsley flakes

Garlic Ranch Dressing

    4–5 tablespoons dry mix
    1 cup low-fat buttermilk
    ½ cup nonfat mayonnaise
    ½ cup light sour cream

To Make Dressing Mix: Mix all ingredients together and put in glass screw-top jar or plastic container with tight-fitting lid. This will make ¾ cup dry mix, which can be stored for 1 month.

To Make Garlic Ranch Dressing: Combine 4 to 5 tablespoons dry mix with remaining ingredients. Refrigerate for at least ½ hour for flavors to blend.

Makes 2 cups dressing.

Low-Fat Tartar Sauce

Two flavorful sauces that help to keep you on the straight and narrow.

¹⁄₂ **cup light mayonnaise**
1 finely minced Cornichon or sour pickle
1 tablespoon minced green onion
1 minced anchovy fillet or 1 teaspoon anchovy paste
1 teaspoon minced capers
1 teaspoon minced fresh parsley
2 teaspoons fresh lemon juice
Garlic pepper to taste

In a small mixing bowl, combine mayonnaise with the rest of ingredients. For best flavor, make one day ahead of serving. Keep refrigerated.

Makes ¹⁄₂ cup.

Low-Fat Roasted Red Pepper Mayonnaise

1 medium roasted red pepper (from a jar)
¹⁄₂ **cup low-fat mayonnaise**
1 clove garlic, minced
2 tablespoons minced green onion
1 teaspoon tomato paste
1 teaspoons fresh lemon juice
Dash of cumin to taste

In a small mixing bowl, combine all ingredients. Keep refrigerated until serving.

Makes ¹⁄₂ cup.

Hint: Great for grilled chicken, fish or in sandwiches.

Red Onion Relish

Double the recipe and give some to a friend — it's a gift of love!

> 1 ½ tablespoons oil
> 2 medium red onions, thinly sliced (about 2 cups)
> 2 small cloves garlic, minced
> 2 cups red wine
> ½ cup fresh orange juice
> ½ cup sugar
> ¼ cup balsamic vinegar
> Salt and pepper to taste

In a non-stick medium-sized skillet, heat oil. Add onions and cook, stirring frequently over moderately high heat, until onions are well-browned, about 6 minutes. Turn heat lower and add garlic. Stir mixture for 1 minute. Add ½ of the wine and simmer, stirring for 10 minutes. Add remaining wine, orange juice, sugar, vinegar, salt and pepper to taste. Simmer mixture over moderate heat until liquid is reduced, about 20 minutes. Remove from heat, cool and refrigerate in covered container. Serve at room temperature.

Makes about 2 cups.

Hint: Use as an accompaniment to grilled meats or as a topping for hamburgers and hot dogs.

Cranberry-Orange Relish

You'll want to add all of these cranberry recipes to your "best" recipe file.

> 1 (12-ounce) bag cranberries, picked over and washed
> 1–2 cups sugar
> ½ cup water
> 2 teaspoons grated orange peel
> ½ cup orange juice
> ½ cup blanched almonds, slivered

Combine all ingredients except almonds in a 1½-quart saucepan and cook over medium heat until the cranberries pop open, about 10 minutes. Do not cover. Skim foam from surface. Add almonds and allow to cool.

Makes 8 to 10 servings.

Cranberry-Apricot Sauce

Eight food testers made this sauce for Thanksgiving. What does that tell you?

> 1 (12-ounce) bag fresh or frozen cranberries
> 1 cup dried apricots, cut in half
> ¼ cup golden raisins
> Peel of 1 orange
> 1 teaspoon cinnamon
> ¼ teaspoon nutmeg
> 1 (11½-ounce) can apricot nectar
> 1 cup sugar

Combine all ingredients in a large saucepan. Bring to a boil over moderate heat, stirring occasionally. Reduce heat to simmer and continue stirring every few minutes for 20 minutes. Cool, cover and refrigerate for up to 1 week.

Makes 6 to 8 servings.

Cranberry-Apple Relish

A wonderful alternative for the holidays.

> 1 (12-ounce) bag cranberries, rinsed and patted dry
> ¼ cup almonds or walnuts
> 1 peeled and cored Delicious apple, cut into quarters
> ¼ cup orange juice
> ½ cup sugar, or more to sweeten
> Cinnamon to taste

Grind or finely chop (can use food processor) cranberries, nuts and apple quarters. Stir in orange juice. Add sugar and cinnamon to taste.

Makes 6 servings.

Cranberry Relish Mold

Refreshing as well as delicious – something different for Thanksgiving.

> 1 (6-ounce) box raspberry gelatin dessert
> 1 cup crushed pineapple, drained but reserve juice
> 1 (12-ounce) package cranberries, washed and picked over
> 2–3 medium apples, cored with skin on
> 2–3 medium oranges, peeled, sectioned, pith removed, leaving just the orange pulp
> 1¼ cups sugar
> ½ cup chopped pecans (optional)

In a large bowl, prepare gelatin according to package instructions, using reserved pineapple juice for the cold water and adding additional cold water to meet recipe requirements. Refrigerate until mixture becomes partially set.

In food processor fitted with steel blade, grind cranberries and apples into small pieces using the pulse button. Add to gelatin and stir. Add pineapple, orange pulp and sugar; mix until thoroughly combined. Pour into a 9" x 13" shallow dish or lightly oiled large gelatin mold. Refrigerate until completely set. Pecans can be used to decorate top of salad rather than mixing into ingredients.

Makes 10 to 12 servings.

Sweet and "Sauer" Kraut

Serve with hamburgers or hot dogs for a real old-time treat!

> **2 medium red peppers, slivered**
> **I large onion, sliced**
> **2 tablespoons oil**
> **2 tablespoons flour**
> **I (28-ounce) can peeled whole tomatoes, chopped**
> **I (32-ounce) jar refrigerated sauerkraut, drained**
> **2 tablespoons brown sugar**
> **Salt and pepper to taste**

Sauté peppers and onions in hot oil in a large skillet over moderate heat until soft. Stir in flour and cook mixture for 30 seconds. Add tomatoes and sauerkraut. Stir constantly until smooth and thick. Turn heat low. Cover pan and cook for 10 to 15 minutes. Stir in brown sugar. Season to taste with salt and pepper. Serve hot.

Makes 8 servings.

Sabrina's Favorite Applesauce

Once you taste homemade applesauce, you'll never want to go back to store bought again.

> **7 pounds Pippin apples, peeled, cored and quartered**
> **I cup raisins**
> **½ cup apple juice**
> **½–I cup brown sugar, or more to taste**
> **I½ teaspoons cinnamon**
> **¼ teaspoon nutmeg**
> **Lemon juice to taste**

Combine all ingredients in a large saucepan. Cook, covered, over low heat until apples are tender, stirring occasionally for about 50 minutes. Remove from heat and cool. Store in airtight container. Best when served at room temperature.

Makes 8 servings.

Spiced Apricots, Pears or Peaches

With very little effort, you'll have an appealing side dish.

3 cups dried apricots, pears or peaches
2½–3 cups water
1½ cups sugar
½ cup cider vinegar
10 whole cloves
2 pieces ginger in syrup, finely chopped
2 sticks cinnamon

Put apricots, pears or peaches in a large saucepan and add water (more if necessary to cover fruit). Soak fruit for 5 minutes and then simmer for 10 minutes. Stir in sugar, vinegar, cloves, ginger and cinnamon sticks. Simmer, covered, for 5 to 8 more minutes, stirring frequently. Serve warm or cold.

Makes 6 to 8 servings.

Jewish-Chinese Pickled Cucumbers

This recipe is a replica of a favorite Chinese restaurant's cucumbers.

8 pickling cucumbers
3 tablespoons seasoned rice vinegar
1 teaspoon sugar
2 large cloves garlic, minced
½ teaspoon pickling spice
Dill weed to taste
Seasoned salt and pepper to taste
1 tablespoon minced green onion

Peel and cut cucumbers into chunks. Put in a glass bowl. Add remaining ingredients. Stir to mix well. Marinate in refrigerator for at least 1 hour.

Makes 4 servings.

Not Grandma's,
but Quick-and-Easy Pickled Beets

If you want Grandma's recipe, use 4 bunches of baby beets, wash, cook, peel, than proceed. Remember, Grandma used salt and cider vinegar.

> 2 (15-ounce) cans sliced beets, drained
> 1 small red or white onion, thinly sliced and separated into rings
> ½ medium lemon, thinly sliced
> ½–1 tablespoon sugar
> 1 tablespoon pickling spice
> 1 teaspoon dill seed
> 1 clove garlic, peeled and left whole
> 1 (12-ounce) bottle seasoned rice vinegar

Put beets, onion slices and lemon slices into a large heatproof glass mixing bowl. In a medium-sized saucepan or heatproof bowl, put sugar, pickling spice, dill, garlic clove and seasoned rice vinegar. Bring mixture to a boil on stove or in microwave oven on high for 3 to 4 minutes. Remove from heat and pour over beets. Cool. Cover with plastic wrap and refrigerate. Drain before serving.

Makes 8 to 10 servings.

Peter's Pickled Peppers

As quickly as you can say the rhyme, you can make these peppers!

8 medium peppers, red, green or yellow
½ tablespoon salt
½ teaspoon pepper
1 bay leaf
½ cup vinegar
½ cup sugar
2 cups water
2 carrots, sliced
2 stalks celery, sliced
2 cloves garlic, minced

Broil or grill peppers until charred on all sides. Put peppers in plastic bag and twist shut. Leave for 10 minutes. Peel skin from peppers under running water. Slice peppers in half lengthwise. Remove seeds and fibers. Set aside.

Combine salt, pepper, bay leaf, vinegar, sugar and water in a saucepan. Bring to a boil. Arrange peppers, carrots, celery and garlic in sterilized 1-quart glass jar. Pour hot liquid over vegetables. Cool and close top. Refrigerate for 6 to 7 days before serving.

Makes 1 quart.

Haroset Sephardic Style (Passover)

Both different — both delicious!

 16 ounces pitted dates
 2–3 medium apples, peeled, cored, diced
 Apple juice
 16 ounces mixed nuts (almonds, walnuts, pecans)
 2–4 tablespoons white vinegar (fruit flavored may be used)
 ½–¾ cup sweet Passover wine
 1 cup applesauce

In a large saucepan, combine dates and apples. Add just enough apple juice to cover. Over moderate heat, bring mixture to a boil. Turn heat lower; simmer until dates and apples are soft. Stir occasionally. Remove from heat and cool. Finely chop nuts in a food processor, one cup at a time. Combine date mixture and nuts in a large mixing bowl. Add vinegar, starting with 2 tablespoons, and taste. Add wine, starting with ½ cup, and add if more is needed. Stir in applesauce.

Makes about 2 quarts.

Haroset with Apples, Cherries and Nuts

 2 medium apples, peeled, cored and finely chopped
 ½ cup dried cherries
 1 cup finely chopped almonds or walnuts
 1 tablespoon orange juice
 1 tablespoon lemon juice
 1 teaspoon cinnamon
 2 tablespoons matzo meal
 3–4 tablespoons sweet Passover wine, or more to taste

In a medium-sized bowl, combine all ingredients in order given. Let flavors mellow for at least 3 hours.

Makes 3½ cups.

Sea Fare:

FISH—BAKED, BROILED, GRILLED & POACHED

Grilled Chilean Sea Bass
with Lemon Caper Sauce

Simple and very good!

> 1 tablespoon oil
> 2 tablespoons chopped green onions
> 1 tablespoon capers
> 1 tablespoon minced parsley
> 1 tablespoon minced basil
> 2 tablespoons white wine
> ½ tablespoon lemon juice
> 4 (1½-inches-thick) sea bass fillets (1½ pounds total weight)
> 1 tablespoon olive oil
> 1 teaspoon seasoned salt
> White pepper to taste
> 1 tablespoon lemon juice

Heat oil in a small skillet. Sauté onions until soft. Stir in capers, parsley, basil, wine and ½ tablespoon lemon juice and sauté for an additional minute. Set aside while preparing fish. Brush fish fillets on both sides with mixture of olive oil, seasoned salt, white pepper and 1 tablespoon lemon juice. Grill fish over hot coals for 4 to 5 minutes on each side. Heat sauce and spoon over fish to serve.

Makes 4 servings.

Grilled Halibut with Shiitake Mushrooms

Easy to make, this recipe scored high in every category – taste, appearance and quality – with the recipe testers.

2 tablespoons light sodium soy sauce
1 tablespoon Chinese rice wine
½ tablespoon sugar
4 (1-inch-thick) halibut fillets or halibut steaks (6 ounces each)
3 tablespoons safflower oil
1 pound fresh shiitake or other mushrooms
2–3 large garlic cloves, minced
½ cup vegetable (or fish) stock
2 tablespoons Chinese rice wine
1 tablespoon light sodium soy sauce

Combine 2 tablespoons soy sauce, Chinese rice wine and sugar to make marinade. Stir to dissolve sugar. Put fish in shallow glass dish and pour marinade over fish. Marinate at room temperature, for at least 30 minutes, turning once.

In a wok, heat oil over high heat until a piece of white onion turns brown. Remove onion and stir-fry mushrooms and garlic for 1 to 2 minutes. Add stock and rice wine. Continue cooking and stirring until mushrooms are soft and liquid has evaporated. Stir in 1 tablespoon soy sauce. Keep mushrooms warm.

Remove fish from marinade and pat dry with paper towels. Grill until fish is easily flaked with a fork. Put fish on platter and top with mushrooms.

Makes 4 servings.

Baked Whitefish
with Pine Nuts and Raisins

Unusual and delicious!

Swiss chard leaves
1½ pounds whitefish or Chilean sea bass, cut into 6 pieces
⅓ cup white wine
½ cup chicken stock (can be made with bouillon cubes)
1 large tomato, chopped
½ cup sliced anchovy-stuffed green olives
1 cup partially cooked, cubed potatoes
⅓ cup golden raisins
¼ cup pine nuts
1 medium pear, peeled, cored and sliced
Seasoned salt and pepper to taste

Lightly grease (or use vegetable oil spray) a 9" x 12" heatproof glass baking dish. Place enough Swiss chard leaves on bottom of dish to cover. Lay pieces of fish on top of leaves. In medium mixing bowl, combine next 8 ingredients. Season to taste with salt and pepper. Spoon evenly over fish. Bake in 350 degree oven for 30 to 35 minutes uncovered.

Makes 4 to 6 servings.

Smoked Salmon and Golden Potato Lasagne

This recipe started a new "traditional" dish for breaking fast – it was so good!

2 tablespoons butter or margarine
1 cup onion slices
½ pound mushrooms, sliced
2 cloves garlic, minced
1 (10-ounce) box frozen chopped spinach, thawed and squeezed dry
Seasoned salt and pepper to taste
1 cup milk (or use ½ cup white wine)
¾ cup heavy cream
2 teaspoons minced fresh dill
1 teaspoon salt
3 pounds Yukon gold potatoes, peeled and sliced ⅛ inch thick into bowl of water
6–8 ounces chopped smoked salmon

Melt butter in a large skillet. Sauté onions and mushrooms over moderate heat until onions are tender. Add garlic, spinach and seasoned salt and pepper. Stir well to combine all ingredients. Set aside.

In a 2-cup measuring cup, combine milk, cream, dill and 1 teaspoon salt. Drain potato slices and pat dry.

In a 9" x 13" x 3" heatproof baking pan, overlap a layer of potato slices. Gently spread half the onion-spinach mixture over potatoes. Sprinkle with half the chopped smoked salmon . Repeat with another layer of potatoes, remaining onion mixture and smoked salmon. Top with last layer of potato slices. Pour milk mixture evenly over top. Cover the pan with foil and bake in 350 degree oven for 1 hour. Uncover and spray potatoes with olive oil cooking spray. Continue baking for 30 minutes or until top is golden brown.

Makes 8 to 10 servings.

Hint: This can be made the day ahead and refrigerated. Bring to room temperature; heat in 350 degree oven for 30 minutes.

Smoked Salmon Hash

This is a wonderful brunch or supper dish.

8 ounces fresh salmon fillet, skinned
Seasoned salt and pepper to taste
3 medium russet potatoes
2 tablespoons fresh lemon juice
6 tablespoons unsalted butter
½ cup finely chopped red pepper
½ cup finely chopped yellow pepper
1 medium onion, chopped
½ teaspoon dried thyme
½ teaspoon dried tarragon
½ teaspoon dried savory
1 tablespoon minced parsley
½–1 teaspoon seasoned salt
¼ teaspoon pepper
6 ounces smoked salmon, cut into small pieces
4 poached eggs, if desired

Trim off dark layer on bottom of salmon. Remove any small bones with tweezers. Cut fillet down the center. Cut each half into 8 slices each (16 altogether). Season both sides with sprinkling of salt and pepper. Cover with wax paper and refrigerate.

Peel potatoes and place in bowl of water to cover. Add lemon juice. Remove potatoes, one at a time, and grate with hand grater through large holes. Food processor grater may also be used. Measure 3 cups of potatoes. Squeeze out all water from grated potatoes. Heat 3 tablespoons butter in heavy skillet over high heat, until almost brown in color. Add potatoes carefully so that butter does not spatter. Spread over bottom of pan. When potatoes begin to brown around edges, start to stir. Lower heat and continue to cook and stir for about 8 to 10 minutes or until potatoes are golden brown. Add 1 tablespoon butter, peppers, onions and seasonings. Continue stirring until vegetables are almost tender. Remove mixture from pan to bowl and keep warm.

Clean skillet and melt 2 tablespoons butter over medium heat. Turn heat to high and add salmon pieces but do not crowd pan. Do in 2 batches if necessary. Cook on one side to golden brown; then turn over.

Reduce heat to medium and add potatoes and other vegetables to pan. Continue cooking for a few minutes, adding smoked salmon to heat thoroughly. Have poached eggs ready to top the hash, if desired.

Makes 4 servings.

Hint: To make easier version of hash, substitute a 24-ounce frozen package of Potatoes O'Brien (a mixture of potatoes, onions and peppers).

Fillet of Sole with Bananas and Almonds

A popular Venice Beach restaurant served this unusual combination of fish, bananas and almonds to its customers for years.

> ½ **cup flour**
> ½ **teaspoon paprika**
> **2 pounds fillet of sole or whitefish**
> **Lemon juice**
> **Seasoned salt and white pepper to taste**
> **Flour**
> **3 eggs, beaten**
> **2 tablespoons oil and butter mixture**
> **2 bananas, sliced**
> **Lemon juice**
> **1 cup sliced almonds, toasted**

Mix together flour and paprika. Sprinkle fish with lemon juice, salt and pepper. Dip fish fillets first in plain flour and then in beaten eggs. Next, dip fillets lightly into flour-paprika mixture. Sauté in oil and butter mixture until golden brown on both sides. Arrange on heated platter. Toss sliced bananas with lemon juice. Sprinkle bananas and toasted almonds over fillets.

Makes 6 servings.

Mediterranean-Style Baked Fish

This flavorful fish brings back memories of sunny island dining.

    1 tablespoon olive oil
    1 large onion, thinly sliced and separated into rings
    3 tablespoons white wine, or more to taste
    2 cloves garlic, minced
    ¼ cup sun-dried tomatoes (not in oil)
    1½ tablespoons capers
    1 (14-ounce) can whole tomatoes, broken into pieces
    6–8 Kalamata olives, pitted and chopped
    1–2 tablespoons fresh basil leaves, shredded
    ¼ teaspoon dried oregano
    Seasoned salt and pepper to taste
    1½ pounds cod, halibut or Mahi Mahi, cut into 1-inch-thick slices (lengthwise)

Heat oil in a large skillet over medium-high heat. Sauté onions until golden brown. Add wine, garlic, sun-dried tomatoes, capers, canned tomatoes, olives, basil, oregano and seasonings. Simmer until mixture starts to thicken, about 10 minutes. Put fish into a greased, shallow 7" x 11" glass baking dish. Spoon tomato-wine sauce over fish. Bake in 450 degree oven until fish is easily flaked, about 30 minutes. Do not overcook.

Makes 4 to 6 servings.

Sweet-and-Sour Salmon

You won't believe what gingersnaps can do for a sauce until you try it.

2 medium onions, sliced
½ cup sugar
½ cup white vinegar
¾ cup water
6 salmon steaks (4 to 6 ounces each)
Seasoned salt and lemon pepper to taste
8 gingersnaps, crushed
¼ cup raisins
¼ cup toasted, sliced almonds (optional)

Sauté onions and sugar in large, heavy skillet over moderate heat until onions are a light brown. Stir in vinegar and water and continue to cook for 10 minutes longer.

Season salmon steaks on both sides with seasoned salt and lemon pepper to taste. Add fish to skillet and continue cooking for 20 to 25 minutes or until fish flakes when tested with a fork. Remove fish and keep warm.

To onions in pan, add crushed gingersnaps, stirring until cookies have melted and mixture is thickened. Add raisins to onion mixture. Spoon onto large serving platter. Lay fish on top and sprinkle with sliced almonds, if desired. Serve immediately.

Makes 6 servings.

Sea Fare

Salmon au Gratin Casserole

You'd be hard pressed to find an easier recipe for a quick supper.

1 cup coarsely crushed croutons
1 teaspoon butter or margarine, melted
1 (5-ounce) package au gratin potato mix
2 cups boiling water
1 (1-pound) can salmon, drained
1 (10-ounce) package frozen peas, thawed
1 cup cottage cheese

Toss crushed croutons with butter and set aside. In a large bowl, mix remaining ingredients and pour into a 1½-quart casserole. Sprinkle with crushed croutons. Bake in 350 degree oven for 30 to 35 minutes or until mixture is set and golden brown.

Makes 4 to 6 servings.

Salmon Spinach Strata

This recipe doubles easily. Great for brunch or lunch.

1 (15-ounce) can salmon
8 slices white bread (may use challah)
½ pound shredded Cheddar cheese (may use low-fat)
1 (10-ounce) package frozen spinach, thawed and drained
4 eggs (may use egg substitute)
2½ cups milk (may use low-fat)
1 tablespoon chopped onion
¾ teaspoon salt
¼–½ teaspoon pepper
¼ teaspoon dry mustard

Drain and flake salmon, reserving liquid. Trim crusts from 5 slices of bread. Cut in half diagonally. Use remaining 3 slices and trimmings to line bottom of greased 8½" x 11" baking dish. Sprinkle with ⅓ of cheese. Spread flaked salmon over cheese. Spread spinach over salmon. Sprinkle with ⅓ of cheese and arrange bread triangles overlapping on top of cheese. Beat eggs, add milk, onion, salt, pepper, mustard and reserved salmon liquid. Pour over bread triangles. Cover and refrigerate at least 1 hour.

Bake in 325 degree oven for 1 hour. Sprinkle with remaining cheese and bake 5 minutes longer. Allow to stand for 5 to 10 minutes before serving.

Makes 6 to 8 servings.

Crisp Skin Salmon

Quick, easy and delicious!

1 (4-pound) salmon fillet, scaled (do not remove skin)
Kosher salt
Seasoned black pepper
Olive oil
½ bunch fresh dill, finely chopped
2 leeks, washed thoroughly, white and pale green part only, finely chopped
1½ teaspoons thyme (½ handful, if fresh)
1 teaspoon rosemary (2 to 3 sprigs, if fresh)
½ cup dry white wine

Sprinkle top side of salmon with salt and pepper. Rub all over with olive oil. In a 9" x 11" x 3" shallow roasting pan, combine dill, leeks, thyme and rosemary. Place salmon, skin side up on top of the herbs. Rub salmon with a little olive oil and a sprinkling of salt and pepper. Pour wine around the fish. Place pan 6 inches under the preheated broiler. When skin looks crisp and well browned (about 12 to 15 minutes), remove from broiler and place on a hot serving platter. Slice salmon into strips.

Makes 8 to 10 servings.

Sour Cream Poached Salmon

Rich in flavor but not in calories.

2 medium yellow onions, sliced ¼ inch thick
Salt, pepper and paprika
2 large salmon fillets, about 12 ounces each
Salt and pepper
Juice of ½ lemon
4 tablespoons light sour cream
4 tablespoons ketchup or chili sauce
1–2 teaspoons white horseradish
Paprika to taste
Seasoned salt and pepper to taste
2 tablespoons butter or margarine
Sprigs of fresh dill
Sprigs of parsley

Place sliced onions in bottom of lightly greased 7" x 11" baking pan. Sprinkle onions with salt, pepper and paprika. Place salmon fillets on top of onions. Season lightly with salt and pepper; sprinkle with lemon juice. In a small mixing bowl, combine sour cream and ketchup with horseradish and mix well. Spread mixture on top of salmon fillets. Sprinkle with paprika, seasoned salt and pepper to taste. Dot each fillet with dabs of butter. Lay sprigs of fresh dill over fish. Add ½ cup water around fish and over onions.

Cover pan tightly with foil and bake in 375 degree oven for 15 minutes. Remove foil and bake 5 minutes longer or until fish flakes easily. Transfer to serving plate and garnish with parsley.

Makes 4 servings.

Pecan-Crusted Salmon

Nut-crusted fish has become the new "in" entrée on many Los Angeles restaurant menus.

¾ cup finely chopped pecans or almonds
¼ cup fine dry bread crumbs
1 tablespoon minced parsley
¼ teaspoon seasoned salt
Dash pepper
3 tablespoons melted butter
Lemon juice
Salt and pepper
4 salmon or red snapper fillets (6 ounces each)

In a small mixing bowl, combine pecans, bread crumbs, parsley, seasoned salt and pepper. Blend in melted butter. Set aside.

Grease a 12" x 14" rimmed baking sheet. Arrange salmon fillets on sheet. Sprinkle with lemon juice, salt and pepper. Spoon and then spread equal amount of nut mixture over top of each fillet. Bake salmon in preheated 350 degree oven until cooked through, about 20 minutes.

Makes 4 servings.

Pescada a La Veracruzana (Fish Veracruz-Style)

Spicy and colorful sauce enhances the red snapper.

2 medium onions, finely chopped
3–4 cloves garlic, minced
Olive oil
4 medium tomatoes, chopped
½ bunch parsley (or cilantro), minced
1 (8-ounce) can tomato sauce
20 pimiento-stuffed green olives
1 (7½-ounce) jar roasted red peppers, cut into pieces
Salt, pepper and oregano to taste
1 whole jalapeño pepper, seeded, minced
1 tablespoon chicken stock mix
3 pounds red snapper or rock cod, cut in large pieces

In a large 12-inch skillet, sauté onions and garlic in about 3 tablespoons of olive oil until onions are soft. Stir in tomatoes, parsley, tomato sauce, olives, roasted peppers, salt, pepper, oregano, minced jalapeño and chicken stock mix. Simmer, with lid slightly ajar, for 20 to 25 minutes.

Add fish to pan; spooning sauce over top and cover for 10 to 15 minutes or until fish is easily flaked. Remove lid; spoon more sauce over fish and serve.

Makes 6 to 8 servings.

Main Courses:
BEEF, LAMB, POULTRY & VEAL

Mom's Grilled Marinated Steak

*"I entered this recipe of my mom, Lillian Goldstein, in **The Better Homes and Gardens New Cookbook,** and they are using it!"* **Lauren J. Dale**

¼ cup soy sauce
1 tablespoon water
1 tablespoon brown sugar
3 black peppercorns
1 star anise
2 small bay leaves
1 small dried hot pepper
2 teaspoons cooking oil
1 teaspoon toasted sesame oil
2 large cloves garlic
4–6 (6-ounce) steaks

In a small saucepan combine soy sauce, water, brown sugar, peppercorns, star anise, bay leaves, hot pepper, oils and garlic. Bring to a boil, stirring to dissolve sugar. Let stand 15 minutes. Strain.

Place meat in a plastic bag set in a shallow bowl. Add cooled marinade. Marinate in refrigerator 8 to 24 hours, turning the bag occasionally. Drain meat. Grill steaks uncovered over medium coals to desired doneness.

Makes 4 to 6 servings.

"Texas-Style" Brisket

Leave it to Texas to come up with something grand!

I (4- to 6-pound) brisket
I cup ketchup
⅓ cup **Worcestershire sauce**
2 cups water
2–8 teaspoons **Tabasco sauce**
I–2 teaspoons chili powder
I teaspoon liquid smoke
I small onion, finely chopped

Cook brisket, uncovered, in preheated 350 degree oven for 2 hours. Remove from oven and drain all liquid from pan. In a medium bowl, mix remaining ingredients; pour over meat. Cover pan with tight-fitting lid (or use foil to cover) and bake in 300 degree oven for 3 hours. Remove from oven; cool and refrigerate.

When ready to serve, take meat out of pan and remove any fat. Slice meat paper-thin. Lay slices in baking pan and spoon sauce over meat. Cover pan; heat in 300 degree oven for 30 to 40 minutes or until hot.

Makes 6 to 8 servings.

Oriental-Style Barbequed Short Ribs

There's something about Oriental-style we just love.

½ **cup teriyaki or soy sauce**
½ **cup ketchup**
¼ **cup brown sugar**
3 tablespoons orange juice
2 teaspoons grated ginger
2 cloves garlic, minced
4 pounds meaty short ribs
Salt and pepper
Flour
2–3 tablespoons oil

Combine teriyaki or soy sauce, ketchup, brown sugar, orange juice, ginger and garlic; set aside. Season ribs with salt and pepper. Dredge in flour. Heat oil in a large skillet. Brown ribs on both sides.

Arrange ribs in single layer in large baking dish (or bottom of foil-lined broiler pan). Pour marinade over ribs. Cover dish or pan with foil. Bake in 350 degree oven for 1½ to 2 hours or until meat is tender. Remove foil and baste with marinade the last ½ hour of baking. Remove ribs from dish or pan. Separate fat from sauce.

Makes 4 servings.

Spicy Orange Beef

Once you get the ingredients ready, the rest goes quickly.

> 1 pound boneless rib steak, sliced in thin strips
> 2 tablespoons soy sauce
> 1 clove garlic, minced
> 1 tablespoon cornstarch
> 2 tablespoons peanut oil, for frying
> ¼ cup slivered orange peel
> 1 large clove garlic, minced
> ½ teaspoon grated fresh ginger or candied red ginger
> 1 cup beef stock
> 3 tablespoons soy sauce
> ¼ cup sherry
> 1 tablespoon red wine vinegar
> ½ cup low-sugar orange marmalade
> 1½ teaspoons chili paste with garlic
> 1–2 tablespoons sugar
> 2 tablespoons cornstarch mixed with 4 tablespoons water

In a medium bowl, combine beef strips, soy sauce, garlic and cornstarch; marinate 1 hour. Heat 2 tablespoons oil in a wok or large, deep skillet just until oil starts to smoke. Stir-fry beef in 2 batches, over high heat, just until meat loses most of its pink color. Remove with slotted spoon. Set meat aside in a bowl.

Mix all other ingredients, except cornstarch and water, in a medium bowl. Turn heat to moderate. Pour orange mixture into a wok or skillet and heat just until sauce comes to a low boil. Stir in cornstarch and water; cook for 1 minute until sauce has thickened and has turned glossy. Add beef and stir until heated through. Serve with rice.

Makes 3 to 4 servings.

Hint: *Meat is easier to cut into thin strips if partially frozen. Chili paste with garlic is found in the Chinese food section of your supermarket or in an Asian market.*

Pepper Beef

Get the preparation out of the way because cooking this only takes minutes.

Beef

      1 pound beef chuck or rib steak
      1 clove garlic, minced
      2 tablespoons soy sauce (may use low sodium)
      1 tablespoon sherry
      1 egg white
      1 tablespoon cornstarch
      2–3 tablespoons oil
      ½ cup chopped celery
      1 cup coarsely chopped green pepper
      1 cup coarsely chopped onions
      2 fresh tomatoes, cut into eighths

Sauce

      2 tablespoons Worcestershire sauce
      2 tablespoons ketchup
      ½ cup chicken stock
      ¼ cup hoisin sauce
      4 tablespoons soy sauce (may use low sodium)
      2 tablespoons red wine vinegar
      1 tablespoon cornstarch
      1 tablespoon water

To Make Beef: Partially freeze meat (about 30 minutes) so that it can be cut into very thin slices. In a large bowl, put meat slices, garlic, soy sauce and sherry. Add egg white and cornstarch. Mix well with meat mixture. Marinate for 2 hours. In the meantime, prepare vegetables in a platter.

To Make Sauce: In another bowl, combine Worcestershire sauce, ketchup, chicken stock, hoisin sauce, soy sauce and red wine vinegar. Put cornstarch and 1 tablespoon water in custard cup and make a smooth paste with your finger (a tip from the famous teacher, Madame Wong). Set aside.

Heat oil in a wok along with a piece of onion (or peeled ginger). When onion starts to brown, add meat (in 2 to 3 batches) and stir-fry until meat just loses its pink color. Remove with slotted spoon to bowl or platter. If needed add a little oil to wok and stir-fry vegetables, except for tomatoes, for 2 minutes. Pour in sauce. Bring to a boil. Pour in beef. Stir-fry 30 seconds. Add tomatoes and stir-fry about 5 seconds. Stir in cornstarch and water; continue to stir until sauce has thickened. Serve with steamed rice.

Makes 4 servings.

Glazed Corn Beef

Corned beef gets a different and new taste and look!

> 1 (5-pound) corned beef
> 1 small can crushed pineapple, not drained
> ½ cup orange marmalade
> 4–5 tablespoons prepared mustard

Put corned beef in a 4-quart stockpot. Cover meat with water. Simmer, covered, 3 to 4 hours. Meat is done when easily pierced with a fork. Remove meat from water and put in a greased baking pan. Combine remaining ingredients in saucepan and cook over medium heat until thick. Spread part of the glaze on meat; bake in 400 degree oven for 1 hour. Baste often with more glaze.

Makes 8 to 10 servings.

Quick Lemon Pepper Lamb Chops

Serve for Chanukah with potato latkes.

> 2 teaspoons lemon pepper
> 2 teaspoons thyme
> 1 teaspoon seasoned salt
> ¼–½ teaspoon garlic powder
> 1 tablespoon olive oil
> 4–6 shoulder lamb chops or 12 rib chops, trimmed of fat

In a small bowl, combine lemon pepper, thyme, seasoned salt and garlic powder. Stir in olive oil. Pour marinade in a glass baking dish (large enough to hold chops in one layer). Turn chops over in marinade. Refrigerate, covered for 2 hours, or at room temperature for 1 hour. Broil or grill, 5 to 6 minutes per side, turning once. Brush with any extra marinade.

Makes 4 to 6 servings.

Lamb Kabobs with
Lemon-Apricot Chutney

Lemon and apricot are perfect flavors to go with lamb.

Chutney
> 1 lemon
> 2 Granny Smith apples (about ¾ pound)
> ¾ cup dried apricots, cut into pieces
> ⅔ cup golden raisins
> ⅔ cup chopped onions
> 1 cup brown sugar, packed
> ⅔ cup cider vinegar
> 2–3 cloves garlic, minced
> ½ teaspoon ground ginger
> ¼ teaspoon cinnamon
> ¼ teaspoon chili powder
> Dash red pepper flakes (optional)

Kabobs
> 3 large garlic cloves, mashed
> 1½–2 teaspoons salt, or to taste
> ½ teaspoon black pepper
> 2½ pounds lamb, cut into bite-sized pieces
> Mushrooms, tomatoes and peppers (optional)

To Make Chutney: Cut ends from lemon and discard; then, cut lemon into 8 wedges. Thinly slice each wedge crosswise. Place in a 2-quart saucepan. Peel, core and dice apples; add to saucepan. Add apricots, raisins, onions, brown sugar, vinegar, garlic, ginger, cinnamon, chili powder and red pepper flakes. Cook over low heat until mixture is thick, 30 to 40 minutes, stirring frequently to prevent burning. Remove pan from heat and cool. Spoon into bowl or jar. Cover and refrigerate up to 1 week.

Makes 2 cups.

To Make Kabobs: Place garlic, salt and pepper in a small bowl and crush with pestle or back of spoon to make a paste. Rub lamb on both sides with paste. Thread lamb on skewers and place on foil-lined broiling pan; broil each side 4 to 5 minutes (medium-rare). Place kabobs on a serving platter. Garnish each kabob with chutney. Can also skewer mushrooms, tomatoes and red, yellow or green peppers, and broil as above.

Makes 4 servings.

Lamb Mrouzia

The best tasting stew we've had in a long time.

> ½ **cup honey**
> ¼ **cup margarine, melted**
> **I teaspoon freshly ground black pepper**
> **2 teaspoons freshly grated ginger**
> **2 teaspoons cinnamon**
> ½ **teaspoon grated nutmeg**
> **I (3-pound) boneless lamb shoulder, cut into bite-sized pieces**
> **Flour**
> **Oil**
> **I cup chopped onions**
> **Pine nuts, toasted**

Combine honey with melted margarine and black pepper, ginger, cinnamon and nutmeg. Set aside. In a large skillet, brown lamb (which has been dredged in flour) in small batches in hot oil over medium-high heat. Season with salt as you cook each batch of meat. As meat is cooked, put in a 2-quart casserole.

Cook onions until tender and golden. Add to meat in a large casserole. Spoon honey mixture over meat and onions. Cook, covered, in 350 degree oven for 2 hours or until meat is tender. If sauce is too thin, thicken with I tablespoon cornstarch mixed with I tablespoon water. Return to oven and cook until sauce has thickened. Sprinkle the top with pine nuts. Serve with bulgur pilaf, if desired.

Makes 8 to 10 servings.

French but "Hamish" Lamb Shanks with Creamy Barley

The lamb is wonderful but the barley is "out of this world."

Lamb Shanks

> 4 lamb shanks (about 4 pounds), rinsed and patted dry
> Seasoned salt and pepper to taste
> ½ tablespoon olive oil or olive oil spray
> 2 cups beef or chicken bouillon
> 1 teaspoon dried rosemary
> ½ teaspoon dried thyme
> 2–3 cloves garlic, minced
> 4 tablespoons white wine
> 1 tablespoon olive oil
> 1 cup thickly sliced carrots
> 1 medium onion, chopped (1 cup)
> 2 cups thickly sliced parsnips
> ½ pound large mushrooms, thickly sliced
> Garlic, salt and pepper to taste

Creamy Barley

> ⅔ cup pearl barley
> 4 cups chicken stock
> 2 tablespoons margarine
> Garlic salt to taste
> White pepper to taste
> 1 tablespoon minced parsley

To Make Lamb Shanks: Season lamb shanks with seasoned salt and pepper on all sides. Heat oil (or use spray) in a large, heavy skillet. Place lamb shanks in skillet and brown on all sides over moderate heat. Remove shanks to a 7" x 11" baking pan.

Pour fat from skillet. Combine bouillon, rosemary, thyme, garlic and white wine; deglaze skillet, stirring until mixture comes to a boil. Boil for 2 minutes and pour over lamb shanks. Cover pan tightly with foil. Bake in 350 degree oven for 2 hours. Meanwhile, in the same skillet, heat oil and sauté carrots, onions, parsnips and mushrooms. Season lightly with garlic salt and pepper; cook for 5 to 6 minutes, stirring occasionally. Add to lamb shanks and continue cooking, covered, for 30 minutes. Remove foil and bake for another 10 minutes, basting with sauce in pan. Serve with Creamy Barley.

To Make Creamy Barley: In a 2-quart saucepan, combine barley and stock. Bring to a boil; then turn heat down and simmer, covered, for 40 to 45 minutes. Stir occasionally. Add margarine, seasonings to taste and parsley.

Makes 4 lamb shank servings.

Lamb and Rice Stuffed Tomatoes

Perfect for Sukkot!

        8 medium firm tomatoes
        1 small onion, finely chopped
        2 cloves garlic, minced
        6 tablespoons margarine
        2½ cups cooked rice
        ½ cup ground cooked lamb
        ¼ cup pine nuts
        1 teaspoon salt
        1 teaspoon ground black pepper
        1 teaspoon herb mix, oregano or basil
        2 tablespoons olive oil
        ½ cup tomato puree
        1 tablespoon lemon juice

Cut tops from tomatoes; scoop out pulp and save, leaving a good shell. Drain upside down on paper towel. In a medium skillet, sauté onion and garlic in margarine until onion is soft. Mix in rice, lamb, nuts, salt, pepper, herb mix and pulp from scooped out tomatoes. Stuff tomatoes with this mixture. Arrange in baking dish. Combine oil, tomato puree and lemon juice; pour over tomatoes. Bake in 350 degree oven for 30 minutes, basting occasionally with the sauce.

Makes 8 servings.

Veal Chops with Mushrooms

If you want an outstanding company dish, this is the one!

> 1 cup dried Italian Porcini mushrooms
> 3 tablespoons margarine
> 1 cup sliced carrots
> ½ cup celery
> 1 medium onion, chopped
> 2 sprigs parsley
> 3 tablespoons flour
> 3 cups beef stock
> 2 cloves garlic, minced
> 1 bay leaf
> 1 teaspoon thyme
> ½ teaspoon sage
> 1 tablespoon tomato paste
> 10–12 (2-inch-thick) veal rib chops
> Salt, pepper and flour
> Margarine and oil
> 2 cups thickly sliced mushrooms
> 6 tablespoons Marsala wine

In a small bowl, cover mushrooms with water overnight. Drain and set aside. Heat margarine in a saucepan until it just starts to brown. Add vegetables; stir and cook until vegetables take on color. Stir in flour and continue to cook for a few minutes. Add beef stock to saucepan. Add garlic, bay leaf, thyme, sage and tomato paste. Bring to a boil; turn heat to low and simmer partially covered 1 hour. Strain and measure 2 cups for brown sauce. Set aside.

Season chops with salt and pepper; dredge lightly in flour. Heat 2 tablespoons margarine and oil in a large skillet. Sauté veal chops until golden brown on both sides. Put on a heatproof platter and bake in 350 degree oven for 15 to 20 minutes. In same skillet, add more margarine if necessary and sauté fresh mushrooms until just tender. Add drained Porcini mushrooms, wine and brown sauce; simmer 20 minutes. Spoon over veal chops when ready to serve.

Makes 10 to 12 servings.

Stuffed Brisket of Beef (Passover)

A lot of ingredients but not a lot of work.

1 (6- to 8-pound) brisket
Salt, pepper, minced garlic, paprika and thyme
½ cup boiling water
6–8 matzos (onion flavored), crumbled
4 tablespoons oil
2 small onions, finely chopped
6–8 dried apple slices, chopped
12 dried pitted prunes, chopped
2 tablespoons minced parsley
½ cup toasted almonds
2 teaspoons salt
½ teaspoon ground pepper
4 eggs, beaten
1 package onion soup mix
3 cups water
1 (8-ounce) bottle chili sauce
1 tablespoon brown sugar
1 tablespoon vinegar
1 teaspoon dry mustard

Make a horizontal slit in brisket, forming a pocket. Season meat with salt, pepper, minced garlic, paprika and thyme. Set aside. Pour boiling water over matzos. Soak for 5 minutes; drain. In a medium-sized skillet, heat oil. Add onions and sauté until soft. Add apples and prunes; continue cooking for a few minutes. Remove from heat. Add parsley, almonds, salt , pepper, matzos and eggs. Mix well. Cool and use to stuff pocket in brisket.

Place meat in a roasting pan. In a mixing bowl, combine remaining ingredients and pour over brisket. Cover pan tightly with foil. Roast in 350 degree oven for 2½ to 3 hours, or when brisket is easily pierced with a fork. Cool for 25 to 30 minutes before slicing. Arrange slices in a heatproof platter. Serve with hot gravy from pan (skim off excess fat first).

Makes 12 to 16 servings.

Middle Eastern Braised Lamb Shanks (Passover)

Everything that you want in a Passover entrée is in this recipe.

½ cup dried apricots, chopped
½ cup dried pears, chopped
½ cup dried cherries, chopped
1 cup fresh orange juice
1 cup dry white wine
8 lamb shanks (about 8 pounds)
Seasoned salt, pepper, cumin and thyme to taste
2 tablespoons olive oil
1 medium onion, finely chopped
4 medium carrots, finely chopped
3 large garlic cloves, minced
3 tablespoons minced parsley
3 tablespoons potato starch
3 medium tomatoes, chopped or 1 (14½-ounce) can tomatoes
2 cups chicken or beef stock

In a microwave-safe bowl, combine apricots, pears, cherries, orange juice and wine. Heat on high for 2 minutes in microwave oven; set aside. Season lamb shanks on all sides with seasoned salt, pepper, cumin and thyme to taste. Let stand for 30 minutes. Heat oil in a 10-quart heavy pot (with tight-fitting lid) over moderate heat. Brown meat on all sides in batches. Place meat on a large platter.

To pot, add onions, carrots, garlic and parsley; cook for 5 minutes, stirring occasionally. Remove vegetables from pot and add to shanks. Stir potato starch into pot, scraping tidbits of meat, for about a minute.

Drain any liquid from dried fruit (set fruit aside) and stir liquid into pan along with tomatoes and stock. Bring to a boil and simmer for about 15 minutes, uncovered.

Return lamb shanks and vegetables to pot; cover and bake in 350 degree oven for 2 to 2½ hours or until lamb is easily pierced with a fork. Remove meat and vegetables to a platter.

Over high heat, bring braising liquid to a boil; skim off any fat that rises to the surface. Add dried fruit and simmer for 5 to 7 minutes; spoon sauce over meat and vegetables.

Makes 8 servings.

Hint: Can be made a day ahead.

Tzimmes with Brisket (Passover)

A delicious meal all in one pot!

2 tablespoons oil
2 onions, sliced
3 cloves garlic, minced
2 pounds sweet potatoes, peeled and sliced
2 pounds carrots, peeled and sliced
1 (3-pound) beef brisket
⅓ cup brown sugar, packed
1 teaspoon cinnamon (optional)
2 cups dry red wine or water
1 head garlic, separated into cloves, unpeeled
Salt and pepper to taste

Heat oil in a skillet; sauté onions and minced garlic. Place onion mixture, sweet potatoes and carrots in a 9" x 13" roasting pan. Place brisket on top, fat side up. Sprinkle with brown sugar and cinnamon, if desired. Add wine and unpeeled garlic cloves. Season with salt and pepper to taste. Cover and bake in 350 degree oven for 2½ to 3 hours, or until tender. Cool and refrigerate.

Remove unpeeled garlic and accumulated fat that has hardened on top. Cut meat into thin slices across the grain. Reheat in sauce in same pan and serve. This should be made a day ahead of serving.

Makes 6 to 8 servings.

Sweet-and-Sour Cabbage Rolls (Passover)

A wonderful entrée for Passover – and any other time of the year.

        2 large heads cabbage
        2 pounds lean ground beef
        1 medium onion, grated
        3 tablespoons matzo meal
        2 eggs
        2 teaspoons salt
        ¼ teaspoon white pepper
        ½–1 cup water
        2 cups sauerkraut with juice
        2 carrots, sliced
        1 (16-ounce) can crushed tomatoes
        1 cup brown sugar
        1 cup raisins
        1 teaspoon sour salt dissolved in ⅓ cup water

Using a paring knife, remove core from each cabbage. Steam cabbages for 5 to 10 minutes to allow leaves to soften. Drain and carefully pull cabbage leaves apart. In a medium bowl, mix meat with onion, matzo meal, eggs, salt, pepper and water. Place a heaping tablespoon of meat mixture on each cabbage leaf. Fold in sides and roll up leaf.

In the bottom of a 6-quart Dutch oven, layer sauerkraut and juice, carrots, tomatoes, brown sugar, raisins and dissolved sour salt. Bring to a boil and cook for 10 minutes, stirring occasionally. Layer cabbage rolls on top of sauce. Cover with tight-fitting lid. Bake in 350 degree oven for 2 hours. Make at least 1 day before serving.

Makes about 30 rolls.

Hint: Except for Passover, 1 cup crushed gingersnaps can be added to thicken the sauce.

Chicken Marrakesh

Add this to your special "make ahead" file.

> **8 skinless, boneless chicken breasts halves, pounded thin**
> **Salt, pepper, allspice and cinnamon to taste**
> **4 bananas, halved**
> **Ginger marmalade**
> **Flour**
> **Oil**
> **¾ cup ginger marmalade or chutney**
> **1½ teaspoons cornstarch**
> **¾ cup chicken stock**
> **1 cup grape halves**
> **Banana slices**
> **Toasted almonds (optional)**

On working surface, lay chicken breasts on wax paper. Season inside of breasts with sprinkling of salt, pepper, allspice and cinnamon. Place banana half near widest side of chicken. Put small dab of marmalade on banana and roll up. Fasten with toothpicks. Sprinkle with salt, pepper, allspice and cinnamon. Roll lightly in flour.

In a large skillet, sauté chicken in oil until golden on all sides. Combine, marmalade or chutney, cornstarch and chicken stock in a small bowl. Arrange fried chicken in a greased 7" x 11" x 2" baking dish. Drain any excess fat from skillet. Return skillet to heat and stir in marmalade mixture. Stir over low heat until mixture comes to a boil. Boil for 1 minute. Pour over chicken. (Can be refrigerated at this point for one day).

Bake in 325 degree oven for 20 to 25 minutes. Add grapes and bananas just before serving. Spoon sauce over chicken. Sprinkle with toasted almonds, if desired.

Makes 4 to 6 servings.

Corn Crêpes with
Southwestern Chicken Filling

Blintzes with a touch of the Southwest..

Corn Crêpes

⅓ cup flour
⅔ cup polenta or yellow cornmeal
1½ cups liquid non-dairy creamer
3 eggs or egg substitute
Dash garlic salt and white pepper

Chicken Filling

½ pound ground chicken or turkey
½ pound mild or spicy turkey sausage, removed from casing
1½ tablespoons oil
½ cup finely chopped onion
½ cup finely chopped red pepper
2 tablespoons minced cilantro
1 cup corn kernels
1 (8-ounce) can chopped green chilies
1 (8-ounce) can tomato sauce
1 (14½-ounce) can ready-cut tomatoes, drained
1 (1-ounce) package taco seasoning mix

To Make Crêpes: In bowl of electric mixer, combine flour, polenta or cornmeal, non-dairy creamer, eggs, garlic salt and white pepper. Beat until smooth. Refrigerate for at least 30 minutes.

Lightly oil a crêpe pan or small frying pan and heat. Pour ¼ cup of crêpe batter into pan; tilt pan quickly (off the heat) to coat evenly. Cook over medium heat until top looks dull. With a long spatula, flip crêpe over and cook for about 10 seconds longer. Remove to platter. Repeat process using remaining batter.

To Make Filling: In a large skillet, sauté ground chicken and turkey sausage (removed from casing) in hot oil until chicken is ôpaque. Remove to a bowl. To skillet, add onions and red peppers. Cook, stirring frequently until vegetables are golden brown and soft. Add cilantro, corn, chilies, tomato sauce, drained tomatoes and taco seasoning mix. Stir to blend ingredients. Cook for 5 minutes. Remove from heat; combine 1 cup sauce with chicken mixture in bowl.

Put some of remaining sauce in a 9" x 13" baking dish. Save remainder for spooning over top of crêpes. Spoon 2 tablespoons of chicken filling in each crêpe and roll to enclose filling. Place in dish, seam side down. Spoon remaining sauce over crêpes. Bake in 350 degree oven for 25 to 30 minutes.

Makes approximately 12 crêpes.

Variation: You can substitute ½ pound ground chicken or turkey for turkey sausage, if desired.

Palm Springs Palomino Chicken

A favorite dish that is served at the Palomino Restaurant in Palm Springs. The waiter gave away the secret ingredients and we came up with our own version.

1 cup finely chopped onions (1 medium)
1 large clove garlic, minced
1 tablespoon olive oil
4–5 medium Roma tomatoes
2–3 tablespoons minced cilantro leaves (optional)
1–2 teaspoons minced fresh ginger
⅔ cup dried apricots, cut in half
¾ cup apricot preserves
½ teaspoon cinnamon
Salt and pepper to taste

In a 10-inch skillet (or wok), sauté onions and garlic in oil over moderate heat until onions are tender, about 5 minutes. Cut tomatoes in half and put in bowl of food processor. Turn motor on and off until tomatoes are coarsely chopped. Pour into a measuring cup (add more tomatoes to make 2 cups); then add to sauté pan.

Continue cooking onions and tomatoes. Stir in cilantro, ginger, dried apricots, ½ cup preserves, cinnamon, salt and pepper. Stir until mixture has thickened, about 5 minutes. Taste sauce and, if needed, add more apricot preserves for a sweeter sauce. Spoon sauce over grilled or broiled chicken.

Makes 2 cups sauce.

Variation: You can also use this sauce to baste roasted chicken, turkey or lamb.

Chicken Wings in Orange-Tomato Sauce with Polenta

An unusual combination of orange and tomato flavors — but it works.

Chicken Wings in Orange-Tomato Sauce

> 1½ pounds chicken wings (or drummettes or small legs)
> ¼ cup lemon juice
> ⅓ cup orange juice
> 1 tablespoon orange peel
> 2 large cloves garlic, minced
> 1 teaspoon garlic salt
> 1 teaspoon dried basil
> 1 teaspoon dried oregano
> 1 teaspoon dried sage
> 1 teaspoon dried rosemary
> 1 tablespoon olive oil
> ½ cup chopped green pepper
> ½ cup chopped onions
> 1 (14-ounce) can ready-cut tomatoes with onions, pepper, garlic and spices
> Polenta
> Minced parsley

Polenta

> 3 cups water
> ½ teaspoon garlic salt
> ½ teaspoon seasoned salt
> Dash white pepper
> 1 teaspoon dried onion flakes
> ½ cup cornmeal
> 2 tablespoons margarine

To Make Chicken: Place chicken in a 7" x 11" heatproof glass baking dish. In a measuring cup, combine lemon juice, orange juice, orange peel, garlic and seasonings. Pour mixture over chicken and marinate for a few hours, turning occasionally. Remove from marinade and pat chicken dry. Save marinade.

Put a large skillet over moderate heat and add oil. Heat until sizzling. Put chicken in pan (not crowding pieces together) and sauté until golden on all sides, about 15 minutes. Remove chicken to platter. Drain all but 1 tablespoon of fat from skillet. Sauté peppers and onions until tender. Stir in marinade along with tomatoes and cook until mixture comes to a boil. Cook for a few minutes.

Return chicken to pan, lowering heat to simmer. Partially cover and simmer for another 20 to 30 minutes or until chicken is tender. Spoon cooked polenta in a serving bowl. Pour chicken and sauce over top. Sprinkle with minced parsley.

To Make Polenta: In a large saucepan, bring water to a boil. Add garlic salt, seasoned salt, white pepper and dried onion flakes. Slowly stir in cornmeal. Turn heat to simmer and continue to stir until mixture is smooth and has thickened. Blend in margarine.

Makes 4 servings.

Honey Mustard Chicken Breasts

You can never have too many chicken recipes, especially when they're this good!

> **4 large boneless chicken breast halves**
> **Garlic powder to taste**
> **Salt and pepper to taste**
> **Paprika to taste**
> **3–4 tablespoons margarine**
> **1 tablespoon honey**
> **1 tablespoon soy sauce**
> **1 tablespoon sherry**
> **1 tablespoon Dijon mustard**
> **1 teaspoon marjoram**
> **Sesame seeds**
> **3 cups cooked rice**

Season chicken with garlic powder, salt, pepper and paprika; place in a baking dish. Melt margarine and add honey, soy sauce, sherry, mustard and marjoram in a saucepan. Pour sauce over chicken and sprinkle with sesame seeds. Bake in 350 degree oven for approximately 1 hour. Serve over rice.

Makes 4 servings.

World's Fair Chicken

Makes a lovely dish for company – creative and colorful!

2 broiler fryers (2–2½ pounds each) cut in half lengthwise (may use chicken pieces)
2 tablespoons margarine
Salt and pepper to taste
1¼ cups orange juice
½ cup raisins or currants
¼ cup chopped chutney (i.e. mango or ginger)
½ cup blanched, sliced almonds
½–1 teaspoon cinnamon
½–1 teaspoon curry powder
Dash of thyme

Arrange chicken halves in a greased, shallow 9" x 13" x 3" baking dish or broiler pan. Dot with margarine, salt and pepper. Bake in 425 degree oven for 15 to 20 minutes or until golden brown.

In a saucepan, combine orange juice, raisins, chutney, almonds, cinnamon, curry and thyme. Simmer for 10 minutes. Pour sauce over browned chicken. Bake in 350 degree oven for 1 hour or until chicken is tender. Garnish (optional) with mandarin oranges, sliced bananas, parsley and serve with condiments such as sliced green onions, coconut chips, preserved ginger slices and banana chips.

Makes 4 to 6 servings.

Hint: Doubles and triples well.

Chicken Chi Chen Itza

A flavorful chicken with Caribbean and Mexican "Cha, Cha, Cha!"

4 cloves garlic, minced
1½–2 teaspoons salt
¼ teaspoon dried red pepper
1 teaspoon oregano
½ teaspoon cumin
1 cup orange juice
⅓ cup lime juice
1½ pounds chicken tenders
Flour
Oil
Seasoned salt and pepper
2 tablespoons oil
5–6 peeled tomatillos, finely chopped
2 tablespoons minced cilantro
1 small onion, finely chopped
1 cup onion rings, sautéed in 1½ teaspoons oil
Orange slices

In a large 9" x 13" oven-tempered glass baking dish, combine garlic, salt, pepper, oregano, cumin, orange juice and lime juice. Add chicken pieces and marinate for at least 3 hours. Drain chicken from marinade (save marinade) and pat dry with paper towels. Dredge lightly with flour and sauté chicken in oil until golden on both sides. Season with salt and pepper. Arrange in a layer in the same baking dish.

In the same skillet, heat oil (if needed) and sauté tomatillos, cilantro and chopped onions until just tender. Add 1 tablespoon flour and blend. Add marinade and stir until well blended. Cook for a few minutes. Taste for salt and pepper. Pour over chicken in baking dish. Sprinkle with sautéed onion rings. Bake in 350 degree oven for 15 to 20 minutes. Garnish with orange slices.

Makes 4 to 6 servings.

Chinese Style Sweet-and-Sour Chicken

Sweet and sour make a winning combination!

1 (8-ounce) can pineapple chunks in heavy syrup
2 pounds boneless chicken breasts or tenders, cut into bite-sized pieces
2 cloves garlic, minced
1 teaspoon salt
½ teaspoon white pepper
1 egg white
2 tablespoons cornstarch
3–4 tablespoons peanut oil
1 small green pepper, cut into chunks
1 small red pepper, cut into chunks
1 medium onion, cut into pieces
1¼ cups chicken broth
4 tablespoons white wine vinegar
2 tablespoons brown sugar
2 tablespoons soy sauce
1 tablespoon hoisin sauce
1 large clove garlic, minced
½–1 teaspoon grated ginger
3 tablespoons cornstarch, mixed smoothly with 4 tablespoons water

Drain pineapple chunks, saving syrup. Set both aside. In a medium bowl, place chicken pieces, garlic, salt, pepper, egg white and cornstarch. Mix with hand to coat chicken. Let mixture stand for 30 minutes.

In a wok, heat 3 to 4 tablespoons oil with a piece of white onion. When onion starts to brown, remove with slotted spoon. Add chicken in 3 batches. Stir-fry each batch (may need to add oil) until golden brown. Remove with slotted spoon to platter. Add peppers and onions to wok and stir-fry a few minutes. Remove to platter.

Combine reserved pineapple syrup, broth, vinegar, sugar, soy sauce, hoisin sauce, garlic and ginger; then add to wok. Bring mixture to a boil over moderate heat. Turn heat down and while sauce is simmering, stir in cornstarch mixture. Stir until sauce is smooth and glossy. Return chicken, peppers, onions and pineapple chunks to wok. Cook and stir for a few minutes longer, just to heat thoroughly. Serve with steamed rice and garnish chicken with crunchy fried Chinese noodles, if desired.

Makes 6 to 8 servings.

Breast of Chicken with Glazed Apples

Mustard and peppercorns are the ying; glazed apples, the yang.

Chicken

 ½ cup Dijon mustard
 1½ tablespoons green peppercorns, drained and mashed
 4 egg yolks
 1 teaspoon parsley
 1 teaspoon chervil
 1 teaspoon chives
 8 skinless boneless chicken breast halves
 Salt and pepper to taste
 Flour
 Fresh bread crumbs
 6 tablespoons margarine
 2–3 tablespoons oil

Glazed Apples

 4 large apples, peeled
 2 tablespoons margarine
 2–3 tablespoons sugar
 1 tablespoon lemon juice

To Make Chicken: In a bowl, blend mustard, peppercorns and egg yolks with herbs. Season chicken breasts with salt and pepper. Dip in flour to coat slightly. Dip in mustard mixture on both sides; then coat with bread crumbs.

Heat margarine and oil in a large skillet. When hot, add chicken a few pieces at a time and cook until lightly browned on both sides. Arrange in a 15"x 10"x 2" baking dish and bake in 350 degree oven for 20 to 30 minutes. Serve with Glazed Apples.

To Prepare Glazed Apples: Cut out core of apples and cut into ¼-inch slices. In a large skillet, melt margarine and stir in sugar and lemon juice. Add apples, and sauté until apples are glazed and golden. Keep warm or reheat to serve.

Makes 6 to 8 servings.

Herb-Scented Mushroom Chicken

This is an easy dish to prepare and great for large groups.

3½–4 pounds chicken (breasts, legs, thighs)
1 teaspoon dried sweet basil
½ teaspoon dried thyme
1 tablespoon flour
1 teaspoon garlic powder
1 teaspoon seasoned salt
1 tablespoon Worcestershire sauce
¼ cup ketchup
¾ cup sherry
½ cup water
4–6 green onions, chopped
½ pound fresh mushrooms, sliced

Place chicken in a single layer in a slightly greased 9" x 13" x 3" baking pan. In a separate bowl, combine all ingredients except green onions and mushrooms. Mix until blended. Pour over chicken. Sprinkle green onions and mushrooms over chicken. Bake uncovered in 350 degree oven for 1 to 1½ hours until tender and brown. Baste with sauce occasionally.

Makes 4 servings.

Hint: *This recipe easily doubles or triples.*

Chicken Paprikash

A wonderful dish for company. Serve with spaetzle.

1 cup flour
2½ teaspoons paprika
¼–½ teaspoon cayenne pepper
½ teaspoon thyme
½ teaspoon basil
½–1 teaspoon seasoned salt
⅛ teaspoon nutmeg
¼ teaspoon ginger
1 teaspoon seasoned pepper
10–12 chicken pieces (breast and thighs), boned and skinned
¼–⅓ cup oil
2 large gloves garlic, minced
2 medium onions, sliced
2½ cups chicken stock
2 tablespoons Worcestershire sauce
½ cup dry sherry
2 cups sour cream substitute, at room temperature
Minced parsley

In a heavy paper bag, combine flour, paprika, cayenne pepper, thyme, basil, seasoned salt, nutmeg, ginger and seasoned pepper. Season chicken pieces lightly with salt and allow to stand for 30 minutes. Shake chicken pieces, a few at a time, in flour mixture. Shake off excess flour.

In a large skillet, heat ¼ cup oil until hot. Fry chicken 4 to 5 pieces at a time, but not crowding the pan, until browned on all sides. Add more oil if needed. Transfer chicken to a 15"x 10"x 2" baking pan.

In the meantime, add a little more oil to the skillet, and sauté the garlic and onions over moderate heat until onions are golden. Remove with slotted spoon and place over chicken. In the same skillet, blend chicken stock, Worcestershire sauce and sherry. Cook, stirring constantly, over low heat. Do not boil. When sauce is heated thoroughly, in a separate bowl, blend in some of the sauce with sour cream substitute and then blend back into sauce. Pour over chicken and bake uncovered in 350 degree oven until chicken is tender, about 50 minutes.

Makes 8 to 12 servings.

Roast Chicken or Duck with Orange-Honey Sauce

Our taste testers gave this sauce the highest score for flavor and appearance!

Chicken or Duck

> **2–3 (5 pounds each) roasting chickens or ducks**
> **Minced garlic or garlic powder to taste**
> **Seasoned salt to taste**
> **Seasoned pepper to taste**
> **1 large orange (for each bird), quartered**
> **Celery leaves (may substitute with cilantro)**

Orange-Honey Sauce

> **1 medium onion, coarsely chopped**
> **1 medium green or yellow pepper, coarsely chopped**
> **2–3 tablespoons margarine**
> **4 cups orange juice**
> **2 cups honey**
> **3 tablespoons lemon juice**
> **1 teaspoon grated lemon peel**
> **Cinnamon to taste**

To Prepare Poultry: Rinse and pat dry chickens or ducks. Season inside with garlic, seasoned salt and pepper to taste. Stuff cavities with orange quarters and celery leaves. Tie legs together to secure oranges inside if necessary. Rub outside of chickens or ducks with garlic, seasoned salt and pepper to taste. Place birds on racks in roasting pans. Roast in oven until birds are brown and legs can be easily moved back and forth.

For chicken, bake in 350 degree oven for 90 minutes, longer if roasting multiple birds. For duck, place in 450 degree oven for 20 minutes if roasting one duck or 35 to 40 minutes if roasting two or more ducks. Prick duck skin wherever there are fat pockets. Turn heat down to 350 degrees and continue roasting for approximately 2 to 2½ hours. Prick thighs with a fork; if juice runs clear, ducks are done. Remove chickens or ducks from oven and cool. Cut into quarters.

To Prepare Orange-Honey Sauce: In a large saucepan, sauté onions and peppers in margarine until soft and glossy. Add orange juice and let mixture come to a simmer. Stir in honey, lemon juice, lemon peel and cinnamon; bring to a boil over moderate heat. Reduce heat to simmer and continue cooking until sauce is reduced by half and thickened, about 20 to 30 minutes, stirring occasionally. The sauce may be prepared ahead and refrigerated. Reheat for serving. If desired, baste chickens or ducks with Orange-Honey Sauce during last 30 minutes.

Makes 6 to 8 servings with 2 birds.

Turkey Spoonburgers

This is a lower fat version of Sloppy Joe's – it's even better the next day!

1 pound ground turkey
1 cup thinly sliced onions
½ cup chopped green pepper
1 cup ketchup
¼ cup sweet pickle relish
1 ½ teaspoons chili powder
1 teaspoon Worcestershire sauce
¼–½ teaspoon seasoned salt
½ teaspoon garlic powder
¼ teaspoon celery seeds
8 hamburger buns, toasted

In a large skillet with high sides, over medium heat, sauté ground turkey, onion and green pepper together until turkey is no longer pink. Drain excess fat. Add ketchup, relish, chili powder, Worcestershire sauce, seasoned salt, garlic powder and celery seeds. Bring to a boil. Reduce heat to low, cover and simmer 20 minutes. Serve on toasted buns. Can also be served in soup bowls without buns.

Makes 6 to 8 servings.

Hint: *Recipe can be doubled and kept frozen. When doubling recipe, cut back a little on ketchup.*

Turkey Picatta

This dish brings raves from family and friends!

> 1 pound turkey cutlets
> Garlic salt to taste
> Seasoned pepper to taste
> ¼ cup flour
> 2 eggs, beaten
> 1 tablespoon water
> 1½ cups seasoned bread crumbs
> Olive oil
> 3 tablespoons fresh lemon juice
> 1 cup chicken stock
> 1½ tablespoons capers
> 1–2 medium lemons, thinly sliced

On a flat surface, lay cutlets between wax paper with approximately 2 inches separating each cutlet. Flatten with the side of a mallet to ¼ inch or less thickness without tearing turkey. Lift top piece of wax paper and sprinkle turkey lightly with garlic salt and pepper. Dredge both sides lightly with flour.

In a shallow bowl, mix eggs and water. Dip floured cutlets in beaten eggs and then in bread crumbs. Heat olive oil (about 2 tablespoons) in large griddle over medium heat. Add 3 to 4 cutlets at a time. Fry until golden brown on both sides. Add more oil if needed to finish remaining turkey. Drain on paper towels.

Arrange slices, slightly overlapping, in a 10" x 15" x 1" baking pan. Squeeze juice of one lemon (about 3 tablespoons) onto griddle along with chicken stock and capers. Stir to scrape up any browned bits from turkey. Pour over cutlets in baking pan. Place a thin slice of lemon on each cutlet. Cover pan tightly with foil. Bake in 350 degree oven for 25 minutes. Remove foil for the last 5 minutes.

Makes 4 to 6 servings.

It's a Winner Turkey Meatloaf

If you have a cholesterol problem, this is the recipe for you — it's low in fat!

1 (8-ounce) jar sun-dried tomatoes
2 cups finely chopped onions
½ cup sliced celery
6 medium cloves garlic, minced
2 teaspoons dried basil
2 teaspoons dried oregano
2 teaspoons dried thyme
3 pounds ground turkey
2 pounds sweet turkey sausage, removed from casing
1 cup minced Italian parsley
3 egg whites
1 egg
½ cup water
½ cup dried bread crumbs
2 teaspoons salt, or more to taste
1 teaspoon pepper, or more to taste

Drain oil from sun-dried tomatoes and save ¼ cup oil. Chop tomatoes and set aside. Heat sun-dried tomato oil in large skillet. Sauté onions, celery, garlic and seasonings until vegetables are tender. Transfer mixture to a large bowl. Mix in ground turkey, turkey sausage, parsley, egg whites, whole egg, water, bread crumbs, sun-dried tomatoes, salt and pepper. Form 2 loaves and place in a 9" x 13" baking pan. Bake in 350 degree oven for 1 to 1¼ hours.

Makes 10 to 12 servings.

Light Turkey Pasta Sauce

You'll never miss "the beef!"

2 tablespoons olive oil
2 pounds ground turkey (may use beef)
1 large onion, chopped
1 medium green pepper, chopped
½ pound mushrooms, cut into quarters
3 medium cloves garlic, minced
2 tablespoons minced parsley
4 cans tomato soup
Seasoned salt to taste
Chili powder to taste
Oregano to taste

In a large skillet, heat olive oil over moderate heat. Sauté turkey until browned. Add onions and green peppers and continue cooking until onions are tender. Stir in mushrooms, garlic and parsley; cook a few minutes longer before adding tomato soup and seasonings to taste. Simmer for 45 minutes. Keep pan partially covered, stirring occasionally.

Makes enough sauce for 6 to 8 servings.

Betty's Turkey Chili with Beans

Zesty and flavorful! This chili has as much spunk as the little lady who shared the recipe.

2 pounds ground turkey
2 medium onions, diced
1 medium green or red pepper, diced
2 cloves garlic, minced
2–3 tablespoons medium or hot chili salsa
1 (28-ounce) can tomatoes
1½ tablespoons chili powder, or to taste
Pepper to taste
Dash Tabasco sauce to taste
1 (15-ounce) can pinto beans, drained

Brown the turkey in a large skillet. Add onions, pepper and garlic. Sauté until crispy tender. Add remaining ingredients; simmer uncovered for 45 to 60 minutes, stirring occasionally. Add beans and heat thoroughly.

Makes 6 to 8 servings.

Chicken with Potato Kugelach (Passover)

"This is a fabulous Passover entrée and a long-standing family favorite." **Thelma Rifkind**

Chicken

>2 large fryer chickens, cut into eighths
>1 cup matzo meal
>1 teaspoon salt
>¼ teaspoon pepper
>½ cup peanut oil
>2 cups chopped onion
>4 cups applesauce
>1 cup orange juice
>2 teaspoons grated orange peel
>1 teaspoon cinnamon
>1 cup blanched almonds, shredded

Potato Kugelach

>2 eggs
>2 cups water
>¼ cup peanut oil
>¼ cup matzo meal
>1 (6-ounce) package potato pancake mix
>1 tablespoon minced parsley

To Make Chicken: Roll chicken parts in a mixture of matzo meal, salt and pepper. Fry in hot oil in a large skillet until brown on all sides. Remove chicken from pan as pieces are browned. When all chicken is browned, drain off all but 2 tablespoons of oil. Add onions to skillet and cook until tender. Return chicken to pan. Mix applesauce, orange juice, orange peel and cinnamon in a measuring bowl; pour over chicken. Cover and bake in 350 degree oven for about 30 minutes until tender; uncover, add almonds and bake for 10 to 12 more minutes.

To Make Potato Kugelach: In a mixing bowl, beat eggs with fork until blended. Add water and oil. Stir in matzo meal, potato pancake mix and parsley. Allow batter to thicken for 3 to 5 minutes. Fill a greased muffin pan (mini-muffin pan is best) with batter and bake in 350 degree oven for 15 to 20 minutes until browned and crusty. Loosen with a knife and remove from pan. Place kugelach around chicken.

Makes 12 servings.

Pasta Possibilities:

GRAINS, KUGELS & PASTAS

The Best Basic Noodle Kugel

This is the "blueprint." Whatever you add makes it yours.

Kugel

>1 pound broad noodles, cooked and drained
>1 cup sugar
>7 eggs, beaten (may use egg substitute)
>3 cups low-fat milk
>2 teaspoons vanilla
>1 (16-ounce) carton low-fat cottage cheese
>1 (16-ounce) carton sour cream (may use light)
>4 tablespoons butter or margarine, melted
>1 cup finely chopped dried fruit

Topping

>1½ cups corn flakes, crushed
>1 teaspoon cinnamon
>½ cup brown sugar, packed
>⅓–½ cup butter or margarine, cut into pieces

To Make Kugel: Mix all ingredients (except for topping) in a large mixing bowl. Pour into a well-greased 9" x 16" x 3" baking pan. Refrigerate, covered, for at least 3 hours or overnight. Remove from refrigerator 1 hour before baking. Bake in 350 degree oven for 1 hour. Remove from oven.

To Make Topping: Combine topping ingredients, except for butter or margarine, and sprinkle evenly over top of kugel. Dot with pieces of butter or margarine. Return kugel to oven and continue baking for an additional 25 to 30 minutes. Allow to cool for 15 minutes before cutting into squares.

Makes about 20 servings.

Variations:

- 1 cup golden or dark raisins
- 1 cup finely chopped dried apricots
- 1 cup diced fresh apples or pears
- 1 cup dried cherries, strawberries or blueberries
- 1 cup drained crushed pineapple or pineapple chunks
- 1 cup drained Mandarin orange segments
- 1½ cups drained fruit cocktail

Fabulous Noodle Pudding

This is definitely rich — but also fabulous!

12 graham crackers, crushed
5 tablespoons butter or margarine, melted
½ teaspoon cinnamon
2 (13-ounce) packages fine noodles, cooked and drained
1 (8-ounce) package cream cheese (may use ⅓ less fat)
1 (16-ounce) carton low-fat ricotta cheese or creamed low-fat, small curd cottage
    cheese
1½ cups sugar
10 eggs
1 (16-ounce) carton sour cream (may use light)
1 tablespoon vanilla
1½ sticks butter or margarine, melted

Combine cracker crumbs, 5 tablespoons butter or margarine and cinnamon in a small bowl and set aside.
Place cooked noodles in a large bowl. Cover with plastic wrap. In bowl of electric mixer, beat cream
cheese, ricotta cheese, sugar, eggs, sour cream and vanilla. Set aside.

Grease two 9" x 13" x 2" baking pans with melted butter or margarine; then pour remaining butter over
noodles and gently mix. Combine buttered noodles with cheese mixture. Pour into pans. Sprinkle
graham cracker crumb mixture over noodle-cheese mixture. Bake in 350 degree oven for 50 to 60
minutes. Allow to cool for approximately ½ hour before cutting into squares.

Makes 18 to 24 servings.

Apple Noodle Kugel

A kugel that says California!

Kugel

> 1 pound noodles, cooked and drained
> 10 tablespoons margarine or butter, melted
> 4 eggs, slightly beaten
> ½ cup sugar
> 1 teaspoon cinnamon
> 2 teaspoons vanilla
> ½ cup orange juice
> 1 cup golden raisins
> 2 large apples, peeled, cored and sliced
> ½ teaspoon lemon juice
> Dash cinnamon

Topping

> 1½ cups crushed cereal
> 4 tablespoons sugar
> ½ teaspoon cinnamon
> Small pieces of butter or margarine (about 3 tablespoons total)

Combine cooked noodles with melted margarine or butter. Add eggs, sugar, cinnamon, vanilla, orange juice and raisins. Stir until well combined.

Pour half of mixture in a greased 9" x 13" x 2" pan. Arrange apple slices over noodles. Sprinkle with lemon juice and cinnamon. Cover with remaining noodle mixture. Sprinkle top of noodles with crushed cereal, sugar, cinnamon and bits of butter. Bake in 350 degree oven for 1 to 1½ hours or until golden brown and set. Allow to cool before cutting into squares.

Makes 12 servings.

Spinach Noodle Kugel

Protein, starch and vegetable — all in one dish!

1 (8-ounce) package wide noodles, cooked and drained
4 tablespoons butter or margarine, melted
1 cup chopped onions
1 packet onion soup mix
1 (10-ounce) package frozen spinach, thawed and squeezed dry
1 cup sour cream (may use light)
3 eggs, beaten
French fried onions for garnish (optional)

Place cooked noodles in a large mixing bowl. Add 2 tablespoons of the melted butter. Sauté chopped onions in remaining butter and add to noodles; mix well. Stir in onion soup mix, spinach, sour cream and eggs.

Pour mixture into well-buttered 8" x 11" baking pan. Bake in 350 degree oven for 50 to 60 minutes or until top is golden brown. Garnish top with French fried onions the last 5 minutes of baking, if desired.

Makes 8 to 12 servings.

Pecan-Apple Kugel (Passover)

This is colorful, appealing and very delicious all year-round.

> 8 matzo squares broken into small pieces
> 6–7 large Granny Smith apples, peeled, cored and sliced
> 2 cups chopped pecans
> 1 stick margarine, melted
> 1 ½ cups sugar
> 1–2 teaspoons cinnamon
> Juice of 2 small lemons
> 9 eggs, beaten

Cover matzos with room temperature water until soft, 5 to 10 minutes. Drain and squeeze dry. In a large bowl, combine matzos with remaining ingredients. Pour into a well-greased 9" x 12" x 3" baking pan. Bake in 350 degree oven for 50 to 55 minutes.

Makes 15 servings.

Zucchini-Mushroom Kugel (Passover)

For a change of pace from the usual sweet kugels, try this tasty vegetable kugel.

> 2 onions, coarsely chopped
> 1 ½ tablespoons butter or margarine, melted
> 4 zucchini, shredded
> 8 mushrooms, chopped
> 8 matzos, broken into pieces
> 6 eggs, beaten
> 1 teaspoon salt, or more to taste
> 1 teaspoon pepper, or more to taste
> Garlic powder to taste

Sauté onions in melted butter or margarine until wilted. Add zucchini and mushrooms; sauté until soft, about 5 minutes. Dip matzos in water to soften; then drain well. Remove vegetables from heat. Mix in matzos and eggs. Season with salt, pepper and garlic powder. Spread in a greased 9" x 11" baking dish. Bake in 350 degree oven for 25 to 30 minutes. Test with toothpick to make sure it is done.

Makes 12 squares.

Dried Fruit and Matzo Kugel (Passover)

It would be a shame to only enjoy this kugel once a year!

6 matzos, crumbled
Warm water
2 cups mixed dried fruits (apricots, peaches and pears)
½ cup golden raisins
½ cup orange juice
¾ cup sugar
½ cup white grape juice or wine
2 cups grated apples
4 tablespoons melted margarine
6 eggs, beaten (or egg substitute)
1 teaspoon cinnamon
¼ cup sugar
¼ cup chopped walnuts or pecans (optional)

Run matzos under warm water to soften. Drain. Cut mixed fruits into bite-sized pieces. Soften fruit and raisins in orange juice by microwaving on high for 2 minutes. Allow to stand at room temperature for 10 to 15 minutes. In a large mixing bowl, combine all ingredients except cinnamon and ¼ cup sugar; mix well. Pour into a greased 9" x 13" baking dish. Sprinkle with mixture of cinnamon, ¼ cup sugar and chopped nuts, if desired. Bake in 350 degree oven for 45 minutes, or until set and golden brown. Cut into squares to serve.

Makes 12 servings.

Festive Fruit and Nut Kugel (Passover)

This is so good, you'll want to serve it year-round.

4 cups matzo farfel
2 (16-ounce) cans sliced peaches, drained
1 (10-ounce) package pitted dates (1 cup), sliced
1½ sticks butter or margarine
8 large eggs
½ teaspoon ground nutmeg
½ cup plus 1 tablespoon sugar
1 (8-ounce) container plain yogurt
1 (8-ounce) container cottage cheese with pineapple
½ cup walnuts, chopped
¼ teaspoon ground cinnamon

Grease a 9" x 13" baking dish. Reserve ¼ cup matzo farfel for topping. In a large bowl, combine remaining farfel and 1½ cups warm water. Set aside. Cut each peach slice into 3 to 4 pieces. Reserve ½ cup peaches and ¼ cup dates. Set aside.

In a small saucepan over low heat, melt ½ cup butter or margarine (1 stick). Pour into another large bowl. With a wire whisk, beat in eggs, nutmeg and ½ cup sugar. Stir in yogurt, cottage cheese, remaining peaches and dates. Fold into soaked farfel just until blended. Pour mixture into casserole. Sprinkle with ½ cup peaches and ¼ cup dates.

In the same small saucepan, melt 2 tablespoons margarine or butter. Remove from heat. Into margarine, stir chopped walnuts, cinnamon, 1 tablespoon sugar and reserved farfel. Sprinkle mixture evenly over kugel. Bake in 350 degree oven for 40 to 45 minutes, until kugel is slightly puffed and set. Cut into squares.

Makes 12 to 16 servings.

Party Rice Pilaf with Dried Fruit Topping

A good-looking and delicious party casserole.

       2 tablespoons margarine
       2 cups long-grain rice
       4 cups chicken stock
       ½ teaspoon salt
       ½ teaspoon sugar
       1 (8-ounce) package blanched slivered almonds
       1 (8-ounce) package raisins or dried cherries
       1 (8-ounce) package dried apricots, quartered
       1 (8-ounce) package pitted dates, cut in pieces
       2–3 tablespoons margarine

In a large deep skillet with a tight-fitting lid, melt 2 tablespoons margarine over medium heat. Stir in rice and sauté for 2 minutes. Add chicken stock, salt and sugar. Cook, stirring until mixture comes to a boil. Reduce heat, cover and simmer for 15 to 20 minutes or until rice is tender and liquid is absorbed. While rice is cooking, prepare topping.

In a 10-inch frying pan, sauté almonds, raisins or cherries, apricots and dates with 2 tablespoons of margarine over low heat. Set aside.

When rice is cooked, spoon into a greased 2½-quart casserole. Using a two-prong fork, stir half the nut and fruit mixture into rice. Spread remaining fruit and nuts over top of rice. Cover and keep warm in a 325 degree oven until serving time, but not more than 1 hour.

Makes 8 to 10 servings.

Hint: *If made the day before, remove casserole from refrigerator and bring to room temperature. Loosen rice with a fork. Add ⅓ cup chicken stock. Cover and heat in 325 degree oven for 45 to 60 minutes or until rice is heated through.*

Artichoke Rice with Pine Nuts

Fit for a "company" dinner!

> **2 tablespoons oil, butter or margarine**
> **1 cup pine nuts**
> **2 cups long-grain rice**
> **1 teaspoon salt**
> **½ teaspoon pepper**
> **4 cups vegetable stock**
> **3 (6-ounce) jars marinated artichoke hearts, drained**
> **⅓ cup chopped pimientos (or roasted red pepper)**
> **⅓ cup grated Parmesan cheese**

Put oil in a large skillet (with tight-fitting lid) over medium heat. Add pine nuts and stir until nuts are lightly golden. Remove nuts and set aside. Add rice and stir for about 5 minutes. Add salt, pepper and vegetable stock. Bring to a boil, reduce heat to simmer; then cover and cook until rice is tender, about 20 minutes. Stir in 2 jars of artichoke hearts, pimientos, cheese and ¾ of the nuts.

Spoon into a well-greased 2-quart casserole. Surround edges with remaining artichoke hearts and sprinkle top with remaining pine nuts.

Makes 10 to 12 servings.

Couscous Vegetable Pilaf

Wonderful with fish or chicken. Also good by combining pilaf with leftover meats or poultry.

2 cups boiling water or vegetable stock
1 teaspoon salt
1 cup couscous
2 tablespoons olive oil or margarine
1 large onion, chopped
2 scallions, chopped
1 red pepper, chopped
1 zucchini, chopped
½ cup canned garbanzo beans
½ cup golden raisins
¼ cup minced parsley
Crushed red pepper and salt to taste
Margarine (about 1 tablespoon)

In a large bowl, add boiling water and salt to couscous and cover until all liquid is absorbed, about 5 minutes. In a large skillet, heat oil, add onion, scallions, pepper and zucchini; cook over medium heat until soft. Combine with couscous.

Place in an oven-tempered greased heatproof 1½-quart glass casserole. Stir in garbanzo beans, raisins, parsley, crushed red pepper flakes and salt to taste. Dot with margarine. Bake in 350 degree oven for 20 to 30 minutes. Add chicken stock or vegetable stock as needed to keep fluffy.

Makes 8 servings.

Mushroom-Artichoke Fettuccine

Compatible vegetables in a comfortable setting.

2 tablespoons olive oil
1 pound fresh mushrooms, sliced
4 cloves garlic, minced
1 teaspoon dry thyme, crumbled
1 red or yellow bell pepper, coarsely chopped
1 (9-ounce) package frozen artichoke hearts, thawed, rinsed, drained
1 cup whipping cream
½ cup vegetable stock
⅔ cup frozen baby peas, thawed
½ cup freshly grated Parmesan cheese
1 tablespoon fresh parsley, chopped
1 pound spinach fettuccine
1 tablespoon olive oil
Parmesan cheese

Heat 2 tablespoons olive oil in a large skillet over medium-high heat. Add mushrooms, garlic and thyme; sauté until mushrooms are lightly browned, 6 to 7 minutes. Add bell pepper and sauté for 3 minutes. Reduce heat to simmering and add artichoke hearts, cream, vegetable stock, peas and ½ cup Parmesan cheese. Simmer for 4 minutes, stirring occasionally.

Cook pasta according to package instructions until just tender, but still firm to bite. Drain. Transfer to a large serving bowl and toss with remaining olive oil. Pour sauce over pasta. Sprinkle with parsley and serve. Additional Parmesan cheese can be added if desired.

Makes 6 servings.

Red Pepper and Basil Pasta

A pinch of hot red pepper gives this pasta a lift!

    2 large cloves garlic, minced
    1 cup finely chopped onions
    2 cups red pepper slices (2 medium peppers)
    2 tablespoons olive oil
    1 cup vegetable broth
    2 tablespoons butter or margarine
    ¼ cup finely minced fresh basil
    ½ teaspoon dried thyme
    Pinch dried hot red pepper flakes
    1–2 tablespoons fresh lemon juice
    Salt and garlic pepper to taste
    1 pound cooked pasta, drained
    Freshly grated Parmesan cheese

In a large skillet, cook garlic, onions and peppers in oil over moderate heat until soft. Add vegetable broth and simmer, covered, for 10 minutes. Let mixture stand for 5 minutes. Puree in a food processor and return sauce to skillet. Add butter, basil, thyme, dried pepper flakes, lemon juice, salt and pepper. Keep sauce warm until ready to serve over cooked pasta. Serve with Parmesan cheese.

Makes 4 servings.

Rigatoni with Salmon and Lox in a Cream Sauce

Salmon and lox go Italian!

2 tablespoons butter
Paprika
1½ cups whipping cream
Seasoned salt and pepper to taste
4 tablespoons grated Parmesan cheese
2 tablespoons minced parsley
2 tablespoons basil
¾ pound flaked poached salmon
4 ounces lox
1 (12-ounce) package rigatoni, cooked and drained
1 tablespoon fresh lemon juice
Peel of ½ lemon
1 cup cooked peas or broccoli florets (optional)
Freshly grated Parmesan cheese
Freshly ground black pepper

In a large skillet, melt butter and stir in large pinch of paprika to turn butter a brick color. Add cream, seasoned salt, pepper and Parmesan cheese. Bring to a boil and cook 30 seconds. Turn heat to low and stir in parsley, basil, salmon and lox. Add rigatoni, lemon juice and peel. Stir in peas or broccoli, if desired. Stir until mixture is heated through. Serve with extra Parmesan cheese and freshly ground black pepper.

Makes 4 to 6 servings.

Treasure House of Color:
VEGETABLES

This Goes with Dinner Carrot Ring

A recipe that had to be the forerunner of carrot cake – it's that good!

½ cup vegetable oil
½ cup brown sugar, packed
1 tablespoon orange juice
2 eggs
1 cup flour
½ teaspoon baking soda
1 teaspoon baking powder
¼ teaspoon salt
½ teaspoon cinnamon
⅛ teaspoon nutmeg (optional)
2 cups grated carrots

Combine oil, sugar, orange juice and eggs in 2-cup measuring cup. Set aside. In a large mixing bowl, combine flour, baking soda, baking powder, salt, cinnamon and nutmeg. Gently stir in oil mixture until blended and then stir in carrots. Pour into 1½-quart greased ring mold. Bake in preheated 375 degree oven until set and golden brown, about 55 to 60 minutes. Cool for 15 minutes before removing from pan.

Makes 8 servings.

Hint: *Fill center of carrot ring with minted baby peas for great color combination and flavor.*

Eggplant Dolma

The perfect autumn vegetable for Sukkot.

10–12 small Japanese eggplants
4 tablespoons olive oil
1 cup long-grain rice
2 cups chopped onions
2 tablespoons pine nuts
1 teaspoon salt
½ cup chopped tomato
2 tablespoons currants or raisins
Dash each, pepper, allspice and dill
Dash dried or fresh mint leaves
1½ cups boiling water
Olive oil
Salt

Remove stems from eggplants. Cut in half and use an apple corer to hollow out centers, leaving a shell about ½ inch thick.

In a large frying pan, heat olive oil. Add rice, onions, pine nuts and salt; stir over medium heat until onions are golden brown. Add tomato, currants and seasonings. Then add 1 cup boiling water. Cover pan and cook over low heat until water is absorbed, about 12 to 15 minutes. Remove from heat and cool.

Lightly fill eggplant with mixture. Cover ends of eggplant with small pieces of foil. Arrange close together in a heavy cooking pan. Sprinkle with olive oil and salt. Pour remaining ½ cup boiling water around insides of pan. Cover and simmer until tender, about 20 to 25 minutes, adding water if needed. Cool in pan. These are served warm.

Makes 5 to 10 servings.

Spicy Sweet Eggplant
(A Jewish Version of Ratatouille)

A good vegetable to serve with grilled lamb or chicken.

1 medium eggplant (1¼ pounds)
Salt
1 medium onion, cut into ¼-inch slices
1 large clove garlic, minced
½ teaspoon basil
½ teaspoon thyme
2–3 tablespoons peanut oil
½ teaspoon seasoned salt, or to taste
½ teaspoon seasoned pepper, or to taste
1½–2 tablespoons fresh lemon juice
¼ cup mango chutney or tomato ketchup

Cut eggplant into 1-inch-thick slices. Sprinkle with salt and let stand for 20 minutes. Pat dry. Cut each slice into 1-inch-wide pieces. Put into a bowl with onions, garlic, basil and thyme. Toss to mix.

In a large skillet, heat the oil until it starts to smoke (or oil shimmers). Add eggplant mixture and stir for about 3 minutes. Reduce heat to medium and stir until eggplant is tender and browned. Remove pan from heat and add the remaining ingredients. Can be served hot, chilled or at room temperature.

Makes 4 servings.

Stuffed Eggplant Latkes

A well-known Italian restaurant serves a small version of this on its antipasti table.

2 tablespoons flour
½ teaspoon baking powder
Salt to taste
1 egg
⅓ cup milk
1 tablespoon oil
1 large eggplant
Salt
Flour
¼ cup vegetable oil
1 cup shredded mozzarella cheese
½ cup grated Parmesan cheese
½ cup ricotta or hoop cheese
1 egg
1 tablespoon minced parsley
1 tablespoon minced fresh basil or 1 teaspoon dried basil
Pepper and nutmeg to taste
1½ cups marinara sauce (purchased or homemade)

Combine flour, baking powder and salt in a large mixing bowl. In a smaller bowl, combine egg, milk and oil. Gradually stir egg mixture into flour mixture, beating until smooth. Set batter aside.

Slice eggplant in half lengthwise. Starting from cut side, cut thin slices, about ¼ inch thick. Salt lightly and let stand for 20 minutes. Pat dry with paper towel. Lightly dredge eggplant slices in flour and then dip into batter. Sauté in hot oil on large griddle. Just fry a few at a time until lightly brown on both sides. Drain on paper towels. Cool.

In a mixing bowl, combine mozzarella, Parmesan and ricotta cheeses. Stir in egg, parsley, basil and then season to taste with pepper and nutmeg. Chill until firm. Lay eggplant slices on flat surface. Place a heaping tablespoon of cheese filling at one end of slice and roll up. Secure with toothpick, if necessary. Place seam side down in 7" x 11" greased baking pan. Spoon on 1½ cups of your favorite marinara sauce. Bake in 375 degree oven for 15 to 20 minutes, until hot and bubbling.

Makes 6 to 8 servings.

Grandma Marie Lee's Baked Corn Soufflé

And everyone loved her after tasting her corn soufflé!

4 tablespoons butter
3 tablespoons flour
2 cups milk (may use low-fat)
4 cups canned corn, drained (may use frozen corn, defrosted and drained)
2 tablespoons sugar
2 teaspoons salt
¼ teaspoon pepper
Dash Tabasco sauce (optional)
4 eggs, well beaten
Grated Cheddar cheese (optional)

Melt butter in a large skillet over low heat. Stir in flour until smooth. Remove from heat and whisk in milk until mixture is well blended. Stir constantly over moderate heat until sauce comes to a boil; then lower heat and continue to stir for one minute.

Remove from heat and stir in corn, sugar, salt, pepper and dash of Tabasco, if desired. Add well-beaten eggs and pour into a greased 2-quart baking dish, leaving enough room at the top for corn to rise slightly. Bake in 350 degree oven for 25 minutes. Sprinkle with Cheddar cheese and continue baking for 10 minutes. (If not using cheese, bake for total of 35 minutes.)

Makes 6 to 8 servings.

Hint: This recipe doubles easily, but longer cooking time is required.

Eggplant and Zucchini Pie

A vegetarian favorite for your next buffet get-together.

1 medium onion, chopped
2 cloves garlic, minced
1 medium eggplant, peeled and cubed
2 large zucchini, peeled and sliced
1/4 cup olive oil
4 medium tomatoes, chopped in food processor
3 eggs
1 tablespoon minced parsley
1 teaspoon dried basil or 2 tablespoons fresh
1/2 teaspoon oregano
Salt and pepper to taste
1 partially baked 9-inch pie shell
1/4 pound mozzarella cheese, sliced
1/2 cup grated Parmesan cheese

In a large skillet, sauté onion, garlic, eggplant and zucchini in oil. Add tomatoes, eggs, parsley, basil, oregano, salt and pepper; cook mixture over medium heat until vegetables are soft. Spoon half of vegetable mixture over partially baked pie shell. Cover with half of the mozzarella cheese slices. Spread with remaining vegetable mixture. Top with remaining cheese slices. Sprinkle with grated Parmesan cheese. Bake in 350 degree oven for 30 to 35 minutes.

Makes 6 to 8 servings.

Laura's Special Roasted Potatoes

One potato, two potato, three potato, four…make a delicious combination.

> 1 large **White Rose potato**
> 2 medium **russet potatoes**
> 3 medium **sweet potatoes or yams**
> 4 medium **red potatoes**
> ¼ cup **olive oil or olive oil spray**
> **Garlic salt or garlic powder to taste**
> **Seasoned salt and pepper to taste**
> **Pinch of paprika**
> **Sprinkling of fresh rosemary**

Rinse potatoes and pat dry. Slice potatoes approximately ⅛ inch thick. Lay out on greased cookie sheet. In a small bowl, mix olive oil with garlic salt, seasoned salt, pepper and paprika (or spray with olive oil and sprinkle wth seasonings). Brush potatoes lightly and top with sprinkling of fresh rosemary. Bake in 350 degree oven for 20 to 30 minutes. Turn potatoes and brush tops with oil mixture. Continue baking until golden brown and crisp.

Makes 6 to 8 servings.

Creamy Mashed Potatoes

A real crowd pleaser.

> 4 (10-ounce) **baking potatoes**
> 1 (8-ounce) package **cream cheese (may use ⅓ less fat)**
> 1 medium **onion, finely chopped**
> 3 **eggs**
> 1 teaspoon **salt**
> ¼ teaspoon **white pepper**
> 1 (3-ounce) can **French fried onions**

Peel and quarter potatoes; then boil in water to cover until tender. Drain and mash potatoes. Add remaining ingredients except for fried onions. Using an electric mixer, beat until most of the lumps are smooth. Spoon into a greased 9" x 13" casserole dish. Bake covered in 325 degree oven for 30 minutes. Top with French fried onions and bake uncovered for an additional 8 to 10 minutes or until golden brown.

Makes 8 to 10 servings.

Low-Fat Garlic Mashed Potatoes

This is the "hot" mashed potato recipe!

1 tablespoon canola oil
5–6 cloves garlic, minced
1 medium onion, finely chopped
5 medium potatoes, peeled and quartered
1 teaspoon salt, or to taste
1 tablespoon minced fresh dill
Garlic pepper to taste
½ cup fat-free sour cream

Heat oil in non-stick pan over moderate heat. Add garlic and onions; sauté until onions are soft. Set aside. Meanwhile, cover and cook potatoes in boiling water until tender, about 20 to 25 minutes. Drain. Mash potatoes with a potato masher. Stir in onion mixture, salt, dill and garlic pepper to taste. Add sour cream and stir to mix. Serve immediately.

Makes 4 to 5 servings.

Variation: For a different look and taste, puree 1 cup blanched basil leaves and add to potatoes with onion mixture.

Carrot-Cheese Potato Patties

A "Mrs. Gooch's" creation…with our own variation!

> **3 cups mashed potatoes**
> **1 large carrot, grated**
> **½ cup minced parsley**
> **½ cup minced green onions**
> **1½ teaspoons seasoned salt**
> **¼ teaspoon seasoned pepper**
> **3 cups grated Cheddar cheese (may use lower fat)**

Combine mashed potatoes with next 5 ingredients plus 2 cups of the grated cheese. Shape into patties. Arrange in a buttered, shallow baking pan. Bake in 350 degree oven for 20 minutes. Sprinkle with remaining cup of cheese and continue to bake until cheese melts.

Makes 6 to 8 servings.

Sweet Potato Oven Fries

A crispy alternative to "regular" potatoes.

> **6 medium sweet potatoes, peeled and cut lengthwise into 8 wedges each**
> **2–3 tablespoons fresh lemon juice**
> **2–3 tablespoons vegetable oil (may use vegetable oil spray)**
> **Salt and pepper to taste**
> **Dash cinnamon and nutmeg**

Brush sweet potato wedges with lemon juice; then toss with oil. Lay wedges on foil-lined baking sheet. Season with a sprinkling of salt and pepper, then cinnamon and nutmeg. Bake in 375 degree oven for about 25 to 30 minutes.

Makes 6 servings.

Hint: Potatoes can be made ahead of time and left at room temperature for up to 2 hours. Re-crisp in 475 degree oven before serving.

Sherry's Princess Potatoes

A wonderful "company" casserole that can be made a few hours ahead of time.

Potatoes

> 6–8 medium potatoes, peeled
> 2 teaspoons salt
> 4–6 tablespoons butter or margarine
> 3 eggs, plus 2 yolks
> Salt and pepper to taste

Onion-Cheese Filling

> 3 medium onions, sliced thin
> 3 tablespoons butter or margarine
> Salt and pepper to taste
> 6 ounces grated Gruyère cheese

To Make Potatoes: Quarter potatoes and drop into boiling water to cover. Add about 2 teaspoons salt to water. Partially cover pan and cook until potatoes can easily be pierced with a fork. Drain. Mash potatoes. Add butter, eggs, salt and pepper to taste.

In a well-buttered 9- to 10-inch casserole, place a layer of potatoes on the bottom and up sides of casserole, reserving some potatoes for topping. Fill with Onion-Cheese filling and spread with remaining potatoes. Bake in 400 degree oven until puffy, about 20 minutes.

To Make Onion-Cheese Filling: Sauté onions in butter until golden brown. Season with salt and pepper. Combine with cheese.

Makes 8 to 12 servings.

California Sweet Potatoes

Pretty as a picture – perfect for a buffet!

4 medium sweet potatoes or yams, scrubbed but not peeled
Lightly salted water
2 medium apples, peeled and quartered
⅓–½ cup brown sugar
1½ tablespoons cornstarch
Salt to taste
1 cup orange juice
¼ cup golden raisins
¼ cup butter or margarine
3 tablespoons sherry (optional)

Cover sweet potatoes with lightly salted water. Boil until potatoes can be pierced easily with a knife. Cool and peel. Halve potatoes lengthwise and arrange along with apples in a single layer in a 7" x 11" greased baking pan.

In a medium saucepan, mix brown sugar, cornstarch and salt. Blend in orange juice. Add raisins, butter and sherry. Stir while bringing mixture to a boil. Cook until slightly thickened, about 2 minutes. Pour over potatoes and apples. Bake uncovered in 350 degree oven for 20 to 30 minutes. Spoon the sauce over the casserole several times during baking.

Makes 4 to 6 servings.

Pecan-Crusted Sweet Potatoes

A winning combination that's easy and delicious!

Sweet Potatoes

> 1 (28-ounce) can cut yams, mashed (may use 3 cups fresh mashed sweet potatoes)
> ½ cup sugar
> 2 tablespoons butter or margarine
> 2 eggs, beaten (or egg substitute)
> 1 teaspoon vanilla
> ⅓ cup milk (or non-dairy creamer)

Topping

> ⅓ cup melted butter or margarine
> 1 cup brown sugar
> ½ cup flour
> 1 cup chopped pecans

Combine mashed sweet potatoes with sugar, butter, eggs, vanilla and milk. Spoon into greased 8½" x 11" baking dish. Mix topping ingredients together and sprinkle on top of potato mixture. Bake for 25 minutes in 350 degree oven.

Makes 10 to 12 servings.

Corn-Filled Red Pepper Cups

A great accompaniment to any entrée, it looks as good as it tastes!

2 tablespoons butter or margarine
2 tablespoons flour
1 cup milk (may use low-fat)
Salt and pepper to taste
2 cups cooked corn
1 tablespoon minced chives
2 egg yolks
Roasted red peppers (homemade or purchased)
Buttered bread crumbs

In a 1-quart saucepan, melt butter, add flour and blend. Cook for 2 minutes. Remove pan from heat and stir in milk. Return pan to heat and stir mixture constantly until smooth and thick over moderate heat. Add salt and pepper to taste. Let cool. Stir in corn along with the chives and egg yolks.

Grease 8 fluted tartlet tins (2¾ inches across the top) and then line with red peppers cut to fit. Fill with corn mixture. Sprinkle with buttered bread crumbs. Arrange tins on baking sheets and bake in 350 degree oven for 15 minutes or until set. Loosen with a small knife around the sides and serve on a platter.

Makes 8 servings.

Three-Cheese Spinach Bake

This would be a meal in itself!

2 (10-ounce) packages frozen chopped spinach
½ cup evaporated milk
2 eggs, beaten
½ cup ricotta cheese
½ cup crumbled feta cheese
¼ cup grated Parmesan cheese
2 tablespoons minced green onion
1 teaspoon seasoned salt
½ teaspoon pepper
¼ teaspoon nutmeg

Cook and drain spinach thoroughly. Cool slightly before adding remaining ingredients. Mix well. Spoon into greased 1½-quart casserole. Bake uncovered in 350 degree oven for 30 to 35 minutes.

Makes 4 to 6 servings.

Hint: This casserole can be made in the morning, refrigerated and then baked before serving. Add 10 minutes to baking time if refrigerated.

Mushroom Florentine

A favorite with the taste-testers!

> 1 pound fresh mushrooms
> 2 tablespoons butter
> 2 (10-ounce) packages frozen chopped spinach, defrosted, squeezed dry
> 1 teaspoon salt
> ¼ cup chopped onions
> 1 tablespoon melted butter
> 1 cup freshly grated Cheddar cheese (may use lower fat)
> Garlic salt to taste

Rinse and pat mushrooms dry. Slice off stems; sauté stems and caps in butter until brown.

Season spinach with salt; combine with chopped onions and melted butter. Line a 10-inch casserole (1½ inches deep) with spinach. Sprinkle with half a cup of grated cheese. Arrange mushroom caps and stems over spinach. Season with garlic salt. Sprinkle with remaining cheese. Bake for 20 minutes in 350 degree oven until cheese is melted and golden brown.

Makes 6 to 8 servings.

Spinach and Artichoke Casserole

You won't have to beg anyone to "eat their spinach" when you serve this!

> 4 (10-ounce) packages frozen chopped spinach
> 4 tablespoons chopped onion
> 2 (6-ounce) jars marinated artichoke hearts
> 1 teaspoon salt
> ½ teaspoon pepper
> Juice of ½ small lemon
> 2 (3-ounce) packages cream cheese, softened (may use ⅓ less fat)
> 1 cup sour cream (may use light)

Seasoned salt and pepper to taste
⅔ cup grated Parmesan cheese

Cook spinach and drain. Add onion, undrained artichoke hearts, salt, pepper and lemon juice. Mix slightly and put into 2-quart heatproof casserole.

Combine cream cheese and sour cream and blend thoroughly with seasonings. Spoon over spinach, spreading to cover well. Sprinkle top with Parmesan cheese and bake in 350 degree oven for 20 to 25 minutes.

Makes 10 to 12 servings.

Zucchini Pancakes

A vegetarian favorite. Serve with a salad and dessert for a satisfying lunch or dinner.

1 pound zucchini
2 eggs, beaten
2–4 tablespoons flour
Pinch garlic powder
1 teaspoon sugar (optional)
¼ teaspoon baking powder
½ teaspoon salt
¼ teaspoon pepper
Pinch nutmeg

Scrub zucchini and trim ends. Grate zucchini and drain well. Mix zucchini pulp with other ingredients. Drop batter onto well-greased hot griddle. Brown on both sides, turning once. Repeat process using all of the zucchini mixture.

Makes about 2 dozen.

Vegetables

Spinach and Tomato Casserole

A colorful casserole that is easily put together.

> **2 (10-ounce) packages frozen chopped spinach, cooked and drained**
> **1 cup herb stuffing mix**
> **1 cup finely chopped onions**
> **¼ cup melted butter or margarine**
> **¼ cup vegetable stock**
> **¼ teaspoon garlic powder**
> **Salt and pepper to taste**
> **3 eggs, beaten (may use equivalent egg substitute)**
> **2 medium tomatoes, thinly sliced**
> **½ cup grated Parmesan cheese**

In a large bowl, mix well-drained spinach with herb stuffing mix, onions, melted butter, vegetable stock, garlic powder, salt and pepper. Stir in beaten eggs until blended. Spoon into well-greased 2-quart casserole. Put sliced tomatoes over top. Sprinkle with grated cheese. Bake in 350 degree oven for 25 to 30 minutes.

Makes 6 to 8 servings.

Passover Spinach Soufflé

This is a meal-in-itself type of casserole.

> **2 (10-ounce) packages chopped spinach, defrosted and drained dry**
> **1 large onion, chopped and sautéed in 2 tablespoons margarine**
> **4 eggs, beaten**
> **1 pint sour cream**
> **1 pint cottage cheese**
> **2 cups matzo farfel dampened with water and drained**
> **½ cup Cheddar cheese, grated**

Mix first 6 ingredients together. Pour into a greased 2½-quart casserole. Bake in 350 degree oven for 40 minutes. Sprinkle cheese over the top and return to the oven for 5 to 10 more minutes.

Makes 6 to 8 servings.

Zucchini Tortilla Lasagne

A great recipe to make for a luncheon.

Vegetable oil
2 tablespoons chopped onion
2 tablespoons butter
1 (10-ounce) package frozen corn kernels, thawed and drained
1 pound zucchini, peeled, cut crosswise into ¼-inch-thick slices
1 tablespoon butter
1 cup ricotta cheese (or small curd cottage cheese)
2 cups (about ½ pound) grated Jack cheese
1 egg, beaten
1 teaspoon cumin
Salt and pepper to taste
2 cups bottled tomato salsa
1 package 6-inch corn tortillas (1 dozen)
1 (6-ounce) jar roasted red peppers, drained and patted dry
3 tablespoons minced cilantro
¼ cup Parmesan cheese or ½ cup grated Jack cheese

Brush 8" x 11" x 2" baking dish with oil. Set aside. Sauté onions in 1 tablespoon butter and set aside with corn. Sauté zucchini in 1 tablespoon butter for 5 to 6 minutes; then set aside. In a mixing bowl, combine ricotta cheese, Jack cheese, beaten egg, cumin, salt and pepper.

Cover bottom of baking dish with a layer of tortillas cut to fit. Spread with ¼ of the salsa. (If salsa from the jar is too runny, drain for a few seconds before using.) Layer with half the cheese mixture, then half the zucchini, half the peppers, then half the corn mixture. Top with 1 tablespoon minced cilantro. Make a second layer of tortillas and vegetables in the same manner. Top with remaining tortillas, salsa and cheese. Sprinkle with last tablespoon of minced cilantro. Cover pan with foil.

Bake in 350 degree oven for 20 to 25 minutes or until heated through. Allow lasagne to stand, covered, for 5 minutes before serving. Cut into 6 or 8 rectangles.

Makes 6 to 8 servings.

Mediterranean Vegetable Medley

Another vegetable winner!

> **3 small Japanese eggplants, cut into ½-inch-wide pieces**
> **¼ cup olive oil**
> **1 medium onion, sliced and separated into rings**
> **1 clove garlic, minced**
> **½ cup diced red pepper**
> **½ cup diced green pepper**
> **½ cup diced yellow pepper**
> **3 small zucchini, peeled and chopped**
> **½ cup diced celery**
> **2 tablespoons finely minced fresh basil**
> **⅓ cup pine nuts**
> **2 tablespoons dark raisins**
> **1 tablespoon capers**
> **Salt and pepper to taste**
> **½ teaspoon sugar**
> **1 tablespoon balsamic vinegar**

Sauté eggplant in heated oil in a large skillet for 5 minutes. Add onions, garlic, peppers, zucchini and celery. Continue cooking and stirring until all vegetables are tender. Add remaining ingredients and taste for seasoning. Heat thoroughly and serve.

Makes 6 to 8 servings.

Hint: *This develops more flavor when made a day ahead.*

Chili Relleno Casserole

This is a great dish to serve at luncheons. Just add cornbread and salad.

Butter
Cornmeal
½ pound Cheddar cheese, shredded
½ pound Jack cheese, shredded
1–2 (4-ounce) cans green chilies (depending on how hot you like it),
    seeded and peeled
½ cup finely chopped onions
¾ cup milk, scalded
5 eggs, lightly beaten
¼ teaspoon seasoned salt
¼ teaspoon nutmeg
1 tablespoon wheat germ

Butter and coat lightly with cornmeal a 9- or 10-inch baking dish. Place half of Cheddar and half of Jack cheese on bottom of baking dish. Cover with chilies. Sprinkle with onion. Add remaining cheeses. In small bowl, mix milk, eggs and seasonings. Pour over all. Sprinkle with wheat germ. Bake in 350 degree oven 30 to 40 minutes or until set. Let stand 10 minutes before cutting.

Makes 6 to 8 servings.

Hint: *This recipe may be doubled or tripled for a crowd.*

Variation: *Can substitute 1 (6-ounce) jar roasted red peppers, drained and patted dry, for green chilies.*

Vegetarian Chili

One great dish!

    1 tablespoon olive oil
    2 large cloves garlic, minced
    1 cup diced onion
    1 cup diced zucchini
    1 celery stalk, diced
    1 medium carrot, diced
    1 medium green pepper, diced
    1 medium red pepper, diced
    1 tablespoon chili powder
    1 teaspoon salt
    ¼ teaspoon pepper
    1 bay leaf
    1 tablespoon brown sugar
    2 tablespoons minced fresh basil
    1 (15-ounce) can chili beans or kidney beans, undrained
    1 (28-ounce) can crushed tomatoes
    ¾ cup chopped spicy peanuts
    1 cup shredded Cheddar or Jack cheese (optional)

Heat oil in a large skillet and sauté garlic, onions, zucchini, celery, carrots and peppers until vegetables are tender. Stir in chili powder, salt, pepper, bay leaf, brown sugar and basil and cook over low heat 15 minutes. Add undrained beans and crushed tomatoes. Continue cooking, uncovered 20 to 25 minutes longer, stirring occasionally. Add nuts and cheese.

Makes 4 to 5 servings.

Pastry Tray:

CAKES, PIES & PUDDINGS

Candied Carrot Cake

This is the all-time winner of carrot cakes!

Cake

>   2 cups flour
>   2 teaspoons baking soda
>   2 teaspoons cinnamon
>   ½ teaspoon salt
>   3 eggs
>   ¾ cup oil
>   ¾ cup buttermilk
>   2 cups sugar
>   2 teaspoons vanilla
>   ½ (8¼-ounce) can crushed pineapple, drained, save juice
>   2 cups grated carrots
>   3½ ounces coconut
>   I cup chopped walnuts or pecans

Buttermilk Glaze

>   I cup sugar
>   ½ teaspoon soda
>   ½ cup buttermilk
>   4–6 tablespoons butter
>   I tablespoon corn syrup
>   I teaspoon vanilla

Pineapple Cream Cheese Frosting

>   I (3-ounce) package cream cheese, softened
>   3–4 tablespoons pineapple juice
>   4–5 cups sifted powdered sugar
>   I teaspoon vanilla

To Make Cake: Combine dry ingredients together in a large mixing bowl. In another bowl, beat eggs; add oil, buttermilk, sugar and vanilla. Add to dry ingredients, blending well. Mix in crushed pineapple, carrots, coconut and walnuts. Pour into two, well-greased 9-inch cake pans. Bake in preheated 350 degree oven for 50 to 55 minutes. Pour hot Buttermilk Glaze over hot cakes.

To Make Buttermilk Glaze: Combine first 5 ingredients in medium-sized saucepan. Bring to a boil, turn heat down and simmer 5 minutes. Remove from heat and add vanilla. Spoon carefully over hot cakes in pans that have been removed from the oven. After cakes are cool, loosen edges and remove from pans. Put together with Pineapple Cream Cheese Frosting.

To Make Pineapple Cream Cheese Frosting: Combine ingredients in bowl of food processor. Blend until smooth. Use as filling and frosting.

Makes 12 to 16 servings.

Chocolate and Almond Cherry Loaf

This has the same texture as a fruitcake, but with a refreshing new taste.

> **3 eggs**
> **1 cup sugar**
> **2 teaspoons vanilla**
> **1½ cups flour**
> **1½ teaspoons baking powder**
> **2 cups toasted almonds, coarsely chopped**
> **¾ cup semisweet chocolate chips**
> **1 cup pitted dates, cut into pieces**
> **½ cup candied or dried cherries**
> **Amaretto liqueur**

Beat eggs with electric mixer until foamy. Very gradually beat in sugar and vanilla until mixture is smooth. Combine flour and baking powder; stir into egg mixture. Mix in almonds, semisweet chocolate, dates and cherries.

Spoon batter into greased, wax paper-lined and greased again 9" x 5" x 3" loaf pan. Bake in preheated 325 degree oven for 1¼ to 1½ hours, keeping a pan of water on shelf below pan to keep loaf moist. Remove from oven. Brush with Amaretto liqueur. Loosen sides and cool loaf completely before removing from pan. Wrap in foil. Keep refrigerated. Can also be frozen. Defrost in refrigerator before serving.

Makes 12 servings.

Banana Nut Cake

This has to be outstanding. Three wonderful cooks submitted the same recipe!

Cake

> 1½ cups sugar
> ½ cup butter or margarine
> 3 eggs
> 2 cups sifted flour
> 1 teaspoon salt
> 1 cup buttermilk with 1 teaspoon baking soda
> 1 teaspoon vanilla
> 1 cup mashed bananas (2 to 3)
> ½ cup chopped walnuts

Chocolate Butter Frosting

> 6 tablespoons butter or margarine, sliced
> 1½ cups powdered sugar
> 4 ounces unsweetened chocolate, melted
> 3–4 tablespoons chilled milk
> 1 teaspoon vanilla
> 1½ cups powdered sugar, or more

To Make Cake: Cream together sugar and butter or margarine in bowl of electric mixer. Add eggs one at a time, beating well after each addition. Alternate dry ingredients with buttermilk; mix thoroughly. Blend in vanilla, mashed bananas and nuts. Pour batter into 2 greased and floured 9-inch round cake pans. Bake in preheated 350 degree oven for 40 to 45 minutes or until toothpick comes out clean. Cool for 10 minutes and remove from pans. Cool completely.

To Make Chocolate Butter Frosting: In bowl of food processor, put sliced butter or margarine. Turn motor on and off until butter is creamy. Add 1½ cups powdered sugar and turn motor on and process until butter and sugar are very stiff. Add melted and cooled chocolate; turn motor on and off for just a few seconds to blend. Add milk, vanilla and 1½ cups powdered sugar. Process until ingredients are blended and smooth. If not thick enough to spread, add powdered sugar, a tablespoon at a time, and process. Use frosting to spread between layers and over top and sides of cake.

Makes 12 to 16 servings.

Fat-Free Pineapple Carrot Cake

Don't tell anyone it's low-fat until they've tasted it; then they'll have a second helping!

Cake

> 1 1/4 cups brown sugar, packed
> 1 cup fat-free egg substitute
> 1 (8-ounce) container nonfat vanilla or lemon yogurt
> 2 teaspoons vanilla
> 2 cups flour
> 2 teaspoons baking powder
> 2 teaspoons cinnamon
> 1 (8-ounce) can crushed pineapple tidbits, drained
> 1 cup golden raisins
> 2 cups shredded carrots

Light Cream Cheese Frosting

> 4 ounces 1/3 less fat cream cheese
> 2 1/2 cups powdered sugar
> 1/2 teaspoon vanilla
> 1/4 teaspoon almond extract
> 2 teaspoons fresh lemon juice

To Make Cake: In large bowl of electric mixer, combine sugar, egg substitute, yogurt and vanilla. Beat at medium speed until all ingredients are blended well. Put mixer on low speed and gradually add flour, baking powder and cinnamon. Do not overmix. Fold in pineapple, raisins and carrots.

Pour batter into well-greased and floured 9" x 13" baking pan. Bake in 350 degree oven for 35 to 40 minutes. Allow to cool completely before removing from pan. Spread top of cake with thin layer of Light Cream Cheese Frosting.

To Make Light Cream Cheese Frosting: In bowl of electric mixer or food processor, beat cream cheese until smooth and creamy; gradually add powdered sugar and blend. Add and blend vanilla, almond extract and lemon juice. (Add a little more lemon juice if frosting is too stiff to spread.)

Hint: Avoid overbeating. Without fat, cake can become rubbery if beaten too much.

Apple Cake with a
Tunnel of Cream Cheese

A wonderful combination of flavors!

Filling

> 1 (8-ounce) package cream cheese (may use ⅓ less fat)
> ¼ cup sugar
> ½ teaspoon cinnamon
> 1 egg

Cake

> 2 cups flour
> 1½ cups sugar
> 2 teaspoons baking soda
> 2 teaspoons cinnamon
> ¾ cup canola oil
> 3 eggs
> 3 medium apples, peeled, cored and diced
> ½ cup chopped walnuts
> Powdered sugar or Maple Sauce

Maple Sauce

> 1 cup pure maple syrup
> 1 stick (½ cup) butter
> ½ cup heavy cream

To Make Filling: In bowl of electric mixer, combine softened cream cheese, ¼ cup sugar, cinnamon and egg until smooth and creamy. Remove mixture to a bowl and set aside.

To Make Cake: To bowl of electric mixer, add flour, 1½ cups sugar, baking soda and 2 teaspoons cinnamon. Add combined oil and eggs and mix on low until all ingredients are combined into a batter. Fold in apples and nuts. Set aside 2 cups batter.

Pour remaining batter into greased 10-inch tube pan. Pour cream cheese filling over batter; spoon reserved batter over cream cheese mixture, carefully spreading to cover. Bake in preheated 350 degree oven for 60 to 65 minutes or until toothpick inserted in center comes out clean. Cool 15 to 20 minutes; loosen around edges and tube before removing cake. Cool completely. Sprinkle with powdered sugar or serve with Maple Sauce.

To Make Maple Sauce: In a saucepan, bring maple syrup, butter and cream to a boil over moderate heat. Boil for 4 minutes. Serve warm. Can be made ahead and kept for 2 days.

Makes 12 servings.

Apple Cake on the Lower Fat Side

Lower in fat – high in flavor!

> **2 eggs (may use egg substitute)**
> **2 cups sugar**
> **⅓ cup oil**
> **⅔ cup applesauce (without sugar)**
> **1 teaspoon vanilla**
> **2 teaspoons cinnamon**
> **1 teaspoon baking soda**
> **2 cups flour**
> **4 cups chopped apples (do not peel)**

Beat eggs with sugar in bowl of electric mixer until well combined. Mix oil and applesauce together and beat into egg mixture. Add vanilla and cinnamon and beat. Mix baking soda with flour and beat in. Add apples and mix thoroughly.

Grease and lightly flour 10-inch tube pan. Spoon batter into pan. Bake in preheated 350 degree oven for 1 hour and 10 minutes. Cool completely before turning out of pan. Freezes well. For richer cake, increase amount of oil and decrease the applesauce by same amount.

Variation: For Passover, substitute the flour with cake meal.

You Won't Believe It's a Prune Cake

It's almost like eating a prune and lemon compote – but much better!

Cake

 2 cups pitted prunes
 ½ cup (1 stick) butter or margarine, room temperature
 1 cup sugar
 ½ cup brown sugar, packed
 2 eggs
 1½ cups flour
 1½ teaspoons baking powder
 1 teaspoon baking soda
 3 tablespoons unsweetened cocoa powder
 2 teaspoons cinnamon
 ½ teaspoon nutmeg
 ½ cup buttermilk
 1 teaspoon grated lemon peel
 2 teaspoons vanilla
 1 cup chopped walnuts

Lemon Glaze

 1–2 tablespoons lemon juice
 1 teaspoon grated lemon peel
 ½ teaspoon lemon extract
 1 cup powdered sugar

To Make Cake: In a medium bowl, combine prunes with water to cover. Heat in microwave for 2 minutes. Set aside to soften. Set aside 3 tablespoons prune water. Drain and chop prunes.

In bowl of electric mixer, cream together butter and both sugars until blended well. Add eggs and continue beating. In another bowl, combine flour, baking powder, baking soda, cocoa, cinnamon and nutmeg; set aside. To creamed mixture, add chopped prunes, saved prune water, buttermilk, lemon peel, vanilla and nuts; beat together on low speed. Slowly add flour mixture until blended well.

Pour batter into well-greased 12-cup bundt pan. Bake in preheated 350 degree oven for 35 to 40 minutes or until toothpick inserted in cake comes out clean. When cake has cooled for 10 minutes, invert and unmold on plate. Cool to room temperature. Spoon Lemon Glaze over cooled cake.

To Make Lemon Glaze: In a small bowl, whisk together lemon juice, peel, lemon extract and powdered sugar until smooth.

Makes 10 servings.

Fresh Fruit Buttermilk Crumb Cake

. . . .

An old favorite now made with buttermilk baking mix – and it still has that old-time flavor.

> **2⅓ cups buttermilk baking mix**
> **⅓ cup plus 3 tablespoons brown sugar, packed**
> **½ teaspoon baking soda**
> **¾ cup buttermilk**
> **1 large egg**
> **2 tablespoons oil**
> **Grated peel of 1 orange**
> **1 teaspoon cinnamon**
> **¼ teaspoon nutmeg**
> **2 tablespoons butter**
> **⅓ cup coarsely chopped walnuts**
> **1 pound fresh, ripe peaches, peeled and pitted (or use nectarines, plums, apricots or apples)**
> **¼ cup sugar**

In a medium bowl with electric mixer at low speed, blend together 2 cups baking mix, ⅓ cup brown sugar, baking soda, buttermilk, egg, oil and grated peel. Increase speed and beat 2 to 3 minutes longer. Set aside.

In another bowl, combine remaining ⅓ cup baking mix, 3 tablespoons brown sugar, cinnamon and nutmeg. Using fork, pastry blender or fingers, work in butter until coarse crumbs form. Stir in walnuts. Set aside. In another bowl, combine peaches with ¼ cup sugar. Set aside.

Pour half of batter into greased 9-inch springform pan, spreading evenly. Sprinkle with half the crumb mixture. Spread remaining batter over crumb mixture. Arrange peaches over batter. Sprinkle with remaining crumb mixture. Bake in preheated 400 degree oven for 35 to 40 minutes. Loosen edges around cake and cool.

Makes 10 servings.

Ilse's Apple Cake

Just like the apple cake many remember from their childhood!

Crust

2½ cups flour
¼ cup sugar
Peel from ½ lemon
1 cup (2 sticks) butter or margarine, chilled
1½ tablespoons vegetable shortening, chilled
2 egg yolks
1 tablespoon lemon juice
1½ teaspoons vanilla

Filling

5–6 medium apples, peeled and cut into ¼-inch slices
½ cup plus 2 tablespoons brown sugar, packed
1½ teaspoons cinnamon or apple pie spice
Juice from ½ lemon
½ cup raisins (optional)

To Make Crust: In bowl of food processor, put flour, sugar and lemon peel. Whirl for a few seconds to mix ingredients. Slice butter or margarine evenly over flour-sugar mixture; add shortening. Turn motor on and off until mixture is crumbly.

In a small bowl, stir egg yolks with a fork. Add lemon juice and vanilla. With motor running, add liquid to flour mixture through funnel. Stop as soon as dough comes together. Remove from processor.

Form dough into flat disc and refrigerate for at least 1 hour. (Dough can also be frozen.) Remove from refrigerator; cut dough in half. Roll out or press into bottom of 8" x 11" pan. Roll out other half of dough (for top crust) between 2 sheets of wax paper. Lay on cookie sheet and refrigerate along with dough-lined pan until filling is prepared.

To Make Filling: Place sliced apples in large mixing bowl; mix in sugar, cinnamon, lemon juice and raisins, if desired. To assemble cake, remove pan from refrigerator. Spread apples evenly over dough in pan. Take out top crust from refrigerator. Remove wax paper from top. Invert over apples and remove second sheet of wax paper. Press edges to seal. Bake in preheated 350 degree oven for about 1½ hours, until golden. Cool in pan. Cut into squares to serve.

Makes 10 to 12 servings.

White Chocolate Cheesecake

Rich and wonderful!

Chocolate Wafer Crust

      1½ cups chocolate graham cracker or chocolate wafer crumbs
      1 tablespoon sugar
      4 tablespoons melted butter

Cake

      3 (8-ounce) packages cream cheese, softened (may use ⅓ less fat)
      1 cup sugar
      4 extra-large eggs, at room temperature
      1 pound white chocolate, melted
      ½ cup whipping cream
      2 teaspoons vanilla
      Sweetened whipped cream and chocolate leaves for garnish

To Make Chocolate Wafer Crust: Combine chocolate crumbs with sugar and melted butter. Press into bottom and 1½ inches up sides of greased 9½-inch springform pan.

To Make Cake: Put cheese in bowl of electric mixer. Add sugar and blend well. Add eggs, one at a time. Add cooled white chocolate a little at a time. Add whipping cream and vanilla and beat for 10 minutes.

Pour into prepared springform pan. Bake in preheated 325 degree oven for 1 hour and 15 minutes or until toothpick inserted in center comes out clean. Cool and then refrigerate until serving time. Decorate with border of sweetened whipped cream and chocolate leaves. Cake can be wrapped in foil and frozen; defrost in refrigerator.

Makes 12 to 16 servings.

Hint: *Chocolate leaves make a beautiful garnish. To make: Rinse and pat dry about 10 fresh camellia leaves. Melt ½ cup semisweet chocolate with ½ teaspoon oil in top of double boiler or in microwave-safe bowl in microwave oven on high for 1 minute. Blend until smooth for 1 minute. Using a pastry brush, brush thin layer of chocolate on underside of leaf. Place on wax paper-lined flat plate. Refrigerate until ready to decorate cake. Peel leaf from chocolate.*

Chocolate Coconut Macaroon Cheesecake

If you like Almond Joy candy bars, you'll love this cake.

Crust

      2⅓ cups flaked coconut
      2 tablespoons melted butter

Cheesecake

      4 (8-ounce) packages cream cheese, softened (may use ⅓ less fat)
      1 cup sugar
      4 eggs
      1 tablespoon vanilla
      2 tablespoons flour
      ¾ cup whipping cream

Chocolate Ganache and Macaroon Topping

      3 cups semisweet chocolate chips
      1 cup whipping cream
      1 (10-ounce) package soft coconut macaroon cookies
      ½ cup chopped almonds, toasted
      Whipped cream (optional)

To Make Crust: Combine 2 cups coconut and melted butter, mixing well. Press into bottom of a 9½-inch springform pan. Wrap bottom of pan with foil to prevent leakage. Bake in preheated 400 degree oven for 6 to 7 minutes.

To Make Cheesecake: In bowl of electric mixer, combine cream cheese, sugar, eggs and vanilla; beat until smooth and creamy. Beat in flour and whipping cream for 5 minutes. Spoon batter into crust. Bake in preheated 400 degree oven for 15 minutes. Continue baking at 325 degrees for 40 to 45 minutes longer. Cool to room temperature.

To Make Chocolate Ganache and Macaroon Topping: In a microwave-safe bowl, combine chocolate and whipping cream. Heat in microwave oven on high for 2 to 2½ minutes, stirring until smooth. Chill until partially thickened, but mixture is still spreadable.

When cake is at room temperature, spread ½ of Chocolate Ganache evenly over top of cheesecake. Arrange macaroons in a single layer over top of chocolate, cutting to fit as necessary (and splitting macaroons horizontally in half if they are thick). Spread remaining Chocolate Ganache carefully over macaroons.

Sprinkle with nuts and remaining ⅓ cup coconut. Refrigerate until chocolate is set and cake is well chilled, several hours or overnight.

Just before serving, pipe outside edge of cheesecake with a border of whipped cream, if desired. Cut into slices.

Makes 12 to 16 servings.

Annabel's Overnight Cheesecake

It's hard not to raid the kitchen when the aroma wafts through the house.

2 cups macaroon crumbs
2 pounds cream cheese (may use ⅓ less fat)
1½ cups superfine sugar
6 eggs
2 tablespoons flour
1 pint heavy cream
1½ teaspoons vanilla

Press crumbs into bottom of well-buttered 9½-inch springform pan. In bowl of electric mixer, add ingredients in order. Beat after each addition. After last addition, beat about 20 minutes longer.

Cover outside bottom of pan with foil to prevent leakage; pour mixture into prepared pan. Bake in preheated 350 degree oven for 1 hour. Turn off heat and leave oven door closed, taking care not to jar oven. Best to bake at night and remove next morning. Keep refrigerated. Decorate with berries, apricot halves or pineapple slices when ready to serve.

Makes 10 to 12 servings.

Apple Cheesecake

An impressive dessert that will become a tradition.

Crumb Crust

> 2 cups graham cracker or gingersnap crumbs
> 2 tablespoons sugar
> 4 tablespoons butter or margarine, melted
> 1 teaspoon cinnamon

Cheesecake

> 1 (21-ounce) can apple pie filling
> 1 tablespoon cinnamon or apple pie spice
> 2 tablespoons brown sugar
> 4 (8-ounce) packages cream cheese, softened (may use ⅓ less fat)
> 1 tablespoon vanilla
> 1 cup sugar
> 4 eggs
> 1 cup sour cream (may use light)

Topping

> 3 tablespoons butter
> 3 tablespoons brown sugar
> 1 teaspoon cinnamon
> ⅓ cup flour
> Whipped cream or non-dairy whipped topping
> Caramel topping

To Make Crumb Crust: In a mixing bowl, combine crumbs, sugar, melted butter or margarine and 1 teaspoon cinnamon. Press into bottom and part way up sides of 9½- or 10-inch springform pan. Wrap foil around bottom of pan to prevent leakage. Set aside.

To Make Cheesecake: Rinse and drain apple pie filling. In another large bowl, combine apples, 1 tablespoon cinnamon and 2 tablespoons brown sugar. Set aside. In large bowl of electric mixer, beat cream cheese, vanilla and 1 cup sugar until smooth. Beat in eggs, one at a time. Beat in sour cream until mixture is smooth. Turn half of mixture into crumb crust. Spoon apples evenly over layer of cheese. Cover apples with remaining cheese mixture. Bake in preheated 400 degree oven for 15 minutes. Reduce heat to 325 degrees and bake 15 minutes longer.

To Make Topping: In a small bowl, combine butter, sugar, cinnamon and flour. Mix with fork or fingertips until mixture is crumbly. Sprinkle this mixture over cheesecake and bake 45 minutes longer. Cool to room temperature before refrigerating. Serve with whipped cream and a drizzle of warm caramel topping.

Makes 12 to 14 servings.

Fresh Plum Cheesecake Kuchen

Rich, old-fashioned and delicious!

> 1½ cups flour
> ¼ cup sugar
> ¼ teaspoon salt
> 1 stick butter or margarine, sliced
> 1 egg yolk
> 4 cups pitted, sliced, fresh prune plums or peeled, sliced fresh peaches
> ½ cup sugar
> 1½ teaspoons cinnamon
> 1 (8-ounce) package cream cheese (may use ⅓ less fat), at room temperature
> 3 eggs
> ¾ cup sour cream (may use light)
> ¾ cup sugar
> 2 teaspoons vanilla
> 1½ teaspoons grated lemon peel

Combine flour, sugar and salt. With fingers, work in sliced butter until mixture resembles coarse meal. Stir in egg yolk with a fork until a dough is formed. Press evenly into a 9½-inch springform pan. Refrigerate 10 minutes. Bake in preheated 350 degree oven for 15 to 20 minutes until golden brown.

Arrange plums (or peaches) on top of crust. Sprinkle with ½ cup sugar and cinnamon. Bake in 350 degree oven for 15 minutes. Beat cream cheese with eggs, sour cream, remaining sugar, vanilla and lemon peel. Remove pastry from oven. Spoon cream cheese mixture on top. Return to oven and bake for 35 minutes longer until top is set in center when pan is jiggled. Cool; then refrigerate until serving.

Makes 6 to 8 servings.

Toasted Pecan and Poppyseed Cake

Once you've assembled the ingredients, this cake is as easy as using a mix – and the taste is one that you will not forget.

>   3 cups flour
>   2 cups sugar
>   1¼ cups oil
>   4 eggs
>   2 teaspoons vanilla
>   ½ teaspoon salt
>   1 teaspoon baking soda
>   1 (12-ounce) can evaporated milk
>   1 (12½-ounce) can poppyseed filling
>   1 cup chopped, toasted pecans

In bowl of electric mixer, combine ingredients in order given. Mix until batter is smooth. Spoon into well-greased 10-inch bundt pan. Bake in preheated 350 degree oven for 1 hour and 10 minutes.

Makes 12 to 16 servings.

Cappuccino and White Chocolate Pudding Cake

Moist and rich – better than a cappuccino!

1½ cups flour
1 cup sugar
6 teaspoons unsweetened cocoa
3 teaspoons baking powder
½ teaspoon cinnamon
¾ teaspoon instant espresso coffee powder
¼ teaspoon salt
¾ cup low-fat milk
⅓ cup vegetable oil
2 teaspoons vanilla
½ cup coarsely chopped white chocolate
1 cup sugar
3 tablespoons unsweetened cocoa
1½ cups boiling water

In a large mixing bowl, combine flour, sugar, cocoa, baking powder, cinnamon, espresso powder and salt. Using a large wooden spoon, beat milk, oil, vanilla and white chocolate into dry ingredients. Spoon batter into greased 9" x 13" baking pan.

In a small bowl, combine sugar and cocoa and spread over the top of the batter. Pour boiling water over cake. Do not stir. Bake in preheated 350 degree oven for 35 minutes or until top looks done and cake tester comes out clean. Serve warm, spooned from the pan.

Makes 12 to 15 servings.

Holiday Honey Cake

For a sweet year, serve honey cake for Rosh Hashanah!

> 1 cup sugar
> 1 cup honey
> 3 eggs
> ½ cup oil
> 1 cup strong black coffee, cooled
> 1 orange, juice and grated rind
> ½ cup finely chopped nuts
> 2 teaspoons vanilla
> 2 teaspoons whiskey (optional)
> 3¼ cups flour
> 3 teaspoons baking powder
> ½ teaspoon baking soda
> ½ teaspoon ground allspice
> ½ teaspoon nutmeg

Blend sugar, honey and eggs; mix well. Add oil, coffee, orange juice, rind, nuts and vanilla. Whiskey may be added at this time, if desired. Sift dry ingredients together and add slowly into batter.

Spoon into a well-greased, floured and wax paper-lined 9" x 13" pan or two 4½" x 8½" loaf pans. Be sure to use enough wax paper (or aluminum foil) so that it hangs over the sides of the pan in order to lift the cake out easily when baked. Bake in preheated 350 degree oven for metal pans or 325 degree oven for glass pans. The 9" x 13" pan takes about 45 minutes but the loaf pans take longer. Test with toothpick before removing to rack to cool completely. Remove wax paper after taking cake from pans.

Makes 12 servings.

Chocolate Torte with Raspberries (Passover)

A fabulous dessert for chocaholics.

> **14 ounces semisweet chocolate, chopped**
> **½ cup butter or margarine**
> **¼ cup milk**
> **5 eggs**
> **1 teaspoon vanilla**
> **½ cup sugar**
> **¼ cup cake meal**
> **¼ cup seedless raspberry jam**
> **1½–2 cups fresh raspberries**

Grease bottom only of an 8-inch round springform pan. In a medium saucepan, combine chocolate, butter or margarine, and milk. Cook over low heat, stirring constantly, until chocolate melts. Remove from heat and cool for 20 minutes.

In a large mixing bowl, beat eggs and vanilla on low speed until well combined. Add sugar and cake meal; beat on high speed for 10 minutes. Stir chocolate mixture into egg mixture and mix well. Transfer to prepared pan. Bake in preheated 325 degree oven for 30 to 35 minutes, until torte is slightly puffed on outer ⅓ of top. Remove from oven and cool on wire rack for about 20 minutes. (Note: Torte is done even though center will appear underbaked. While cooling, torte may fall in center and may develop a brownie-like, crusty surface on top. This is normal and will look fine when topped with the jam and berries.)

Using a knife, carefully loosen torte from sides of the pan. Cool completely, about 2 to 3 hours. Remove sides of pan. Wrap torte in foil and chill overnight or up to 2 days. In a small saucepan, melt raspberry jam. Cool. Spread jam over top of torte. Cover with fresh raspberries, stem side down. If desired, dust berries lightly with sifted powdered sugar just before serving. Serve at room temperature.

Makes 16 servings.

Hint: *To make this recipe Pareve, substitute milk with half water and half mocha mix. To watch cholesterol, use egg substitute.*

Cinnamon-Apple Cake (Passover)

The best choice for a Passover apple cake!

- ¾ **cup sugar**
- **2 teaspoons cinnamon**
- **5 medium Pippin apples, peeled and sliced**
- **Juice of 1 small lemon**
- **6 eggs**
- 1¾ **cups sugar**
- **1 cup vegetable or safflower oil**
- **2 cups cake meal**
- **2 teaspoons potato starch**
- **Dash salt**
- ¼ **cup sugar**
- **2 teaspoons cinnamon**
- ⅓ **cup chopped walnuts**

In a large bowl, combine sugar and cinnamon; mix with apples and lemon juice. Set mixture aside. Beat eggs with 1¾ cups sugar in bowl of electric mixer; add oil. In a separate bowl, combine cake meal, potato starch and salt; add slowly to egg mixture, blending well. Pour half of batter into a greased 9" x 13" pan. Spread apple mixture over batter. Top with remaining batter. Combine remaining sugar, cinnamon and nuts; sprinkle over cake. Bake in preheated 350 degree oven for 1 hour and 15 minutes, or until cake tests done.

Makes 12 servings.

Deep Dish Apple-Blueberry Crumb Pie

An impressive looking and easy-to-make pie that everyone will love.

Pie

> 1 refrigerated pie crust dough
> 1 tablespoon butter or margarine
> 3½ pounds Pippin apples, peeled, cored, and cut into ¼-inch slices
> 2 pints fresh blueberries (may substitute 2 boxes frozen, thawed and drained)
> ¼ cup sugar

Crumb Topping

> ⅓ cup flour
> ⅓ cup plus 2 tablespoons brown sugar, packed
> ⅓ cup plus 2 tablespoons finely chopped walnuts
> 4 tablespoons chilled sweet butter, cut into small pieces

To Make Pie: Press pie dough gently into a 9-inch deep-dish pie pan. Press together any splits in dough. Refrigerate for 10 minutes.

In a large skillet, melt butter over moderate heat. Stir in apples and cook, covered, about 15 minutes, until apples are tender. Stir occasionally. Sprinkle blueberries over top of apple mixture. Cook, uncovered, about 5 minutes, until liquid evaporates. Remove from heat. Stir in sugar and cool slightly. Set aside.

Remove pie crust from refrigerator and spoon in apple filling. Sprinkle with Crumb Topping. Bake in preheated 375 degree oven (use rack in lowest third of oven) for about 50 minutes, or until topping is brown. Cool on rack. Serve slightly warm with ice cream or whipped cream.

To Make Crumb Topping: In a small bowl, combine flour, brown sugar and walnuts. Cut in butter and rub mixture together with fingers until crumbly.

Makes 8 servings.

Walnut-Topped Sour Cream Apple Pie

Sugar and spice and everything nice in an all-American apple pie!

Pie Crust

> 1½ cups flour
> 3 tablespoons sugar
> ½ teaspoon salt
> ½ teaspoon cinnamon
> 1 stick butter or margarine
> 3–4 tablespoons apple cider
> Beaten egg yolk

Filling

> 1 egg, lightly beaten
> 1½ cups sour cream (may use light)
> 1 cup sugar
> ½ teaspoon salt
> 2 teaspoons vanilla
> ¼ cup flour
> 8–10 large tart apples, pared, cored and sliced

Topping

> ⅔ cup brown sugar
> ⅓ cup granulated sugar
> 1½ teaspoons cinnamon
> ½ cup flour
> Dash salt
> 1½ cups chopped walnuts or pecans
> 8 tablespoons melted butter

To Make Pie Crust: Combine flour, sugar, salt and cinnamon in food processor, using steel blade. Cut butter or margarine into slices over the flour mixture. Turn food processor on and off until mixture is crumbly. Add just enough cider so that dough leaves sides of bowl. Refrigerate dough for ½ hour. Roll out dough and fit into a 10-inch pie plate. Brush with egg yolk and bake in preheated 450 degree oven for 3 to 5 minutes. Set aside for filling.

To Make Filling: Mix egg, sour cream, sugar, salt, vanilla and flour. Add mixture to apples in a large bowl and toss until apples are lightly coated. Spoon into pie shell. Bake in 450 degree oven for 10 minutes; then reduce heat to 350 degrees and cover loosely with foil. When pie has been in oven 30 minutes, spread on topping and continue baking until apples are tender and top is golden brown, about 45 to 50 minutes.

To Make Topping: Mix sugars, cinnamon, flour and salt. Add nuts and butter; blend.

Upside Down Apple Pie

A Jewish lady's version of Tarte Tatin.

> 3 tablespoons butter or margarine
> 1¼ cups sugar
> ¼ cup water
> 6 medium-sized Golden Delicious apples, peeled, cored and cut in half
> ½ teaspoon ground cinnamon
> 1 (10-ounce) package frozen pastry shells, thawed
> Whipped cream or non-dairy whipped topping (optional)

Melt butter in a heavy 10-inch frying pan. Add sugar and water and cook over medium heat until sugar dissolves and begins to bubble. Add the apple halves and continue to cook, turning apples frequently. Cook for about 35 to 40 minutes or until apples become translucent and liquid is the consistency of corn syrup. Remove pan from heat and sprinkle apples with cinnamon. Pour sauce in an ovenproof 10-inch metal pie pan. Arrange apples cut-side down; cool for at least 30 minutes.

Shortly before serving, arrange pastry shells in a circle on lightly floured board, overlapping edges slightly. Roll out to a 14-inch round. Place on top of apples, tucking edges down between apples and pan. Cut vents in top. Bake pie in preheated 425 degree oven for 20 to 25 minutes, or until pastry top is puffed and golden. Cool on a rack for 15 minutes; then use a spatula to loosen crust edges from pan sides. Place a large plate over the pan and invert together; tap the pan bottom if necessary to turn out pie; then lift off pan. Serve warm with whipped cream or non-dairy whipped topping.

Makes 8 servings.

Cecelia's Blue Ribbon Lemon Meringue Pie

This recipe made its way to a Sunkist recipe booklet as the Blue Ribbon Winner.

Flaky Pastry Pie Shell

> 1 cup flour
> ½ teaspoon salt
> ⅓ cup cold shortening
> 2–3 tablespoons water

Lemon Filling

> 1½ cups sugar
> ⅓ cup cornstarch
> 1½ cups water
> 3 egg yolks, slightly beaten
> ⅓ cup fresh lemon juice
> 2 tablespoons butter or margarine

Meringue

> 3 egg whites
> ¼ teaspoon cream of tartar
> Dash salt
> 6 tablespoons sugar
> ½ teaspoon vanilla

To Make Flaky Pastry Pie Shell: Put flour and salt in bowl of food processor, using steel blade. Cut shortening over flour. Turn motor on and off until mixture is crumbly. Add water through funnel and run processor until mixture starts to leave sides of bowl and forms a ball. Roll out dough between 2 sheets of wax paper to ⅛ inch thick and fit into a 9-inch pie pan; flute edges. Cut foil to gently fit in bottom and up sides of pastry-lined pie pan. Weigh down with beans or rice. Bake in preheated 425 degree oven for 15 minutes. Remove beans or rice and foil. Continue baking until crust is golden, about 8 to 10 minutes.

To Make Filling: In a heavy saucepan, combine sugar and cornstarch. Stir water in gradually. Cook over moderate heat, stirring constantly until mixture thickens and boils for 1 minute. Slowly stir some of the hot mixture into the beaten yolks; then blend back into hot mixture. Cook 1 minute longer, stirring constantly. Remove from heat; stir in lemon juice and blend well. Add butter and blend. Pour into baked shell.

To Make Meringue: Beat whites with cream of tartar and salt until frothy and soft peaks form. Gradually beat in sugar, a tablespoon at a time. Continue beating until stiff peaks form. Beat in vanilla. Pile meringue onto hot pie filling, being careful to seal the meringue onto edge of crust to prevent shrinking. Swirl with the back of a spoon to make points. Bake in 400 degree oven for 8 to 10 minutes. Cool slightly in warm place away from drafts.

Chocolate Pecan Pie

The first bite says it all.

       1 9-inch unbaked pastry crust
       3 eggs
       ⅔ cup sugar
       ½ teaspoon salt
       ⅓ cup melted butter or margarine
       1 cup dark corn syrup
       1 cup chopped pecans
       ½–1 cup semisweet chocolate pieces
       Whipped cream for garnish

Keep pastry crust in refrigerator while preparing filling. In a large mixing bowl, beat together eggs, sugar, salt, butter or margarine and corn syrup. Mix in pecans and chocolate pieces. Pour into pastry crust. Bake in preheated 375 degree oven for about 30 to 40 minutes or until nicely browned. Serve warm, topped with whipped cream.

Passover Fruit Compote

A very festive fruit dessert. If you want to finish the leftover macaroons, put them in this compote – they'll be right at home.

> 1 (16-ounce) can Bing cherries, drained
> 2 (8-ounce) cans Mandarin oranges, drained
> 1 (16-ounce) can peach halves, drained
> 1 (16-ounce) can pineapple (chunks or crushed), drained
> 1 (16-ounce) can pear halves, drained
> 1 dozen Passover macaroons
> ½ cup slivered almonds
> 1 cup sweet red wine

Layer drained fruit in a well-greased 9" x 13" shallow baking dish, sprinkling broken bits of macaroons and slivered almonds between layers. Over the top layer, pour wine. Bake in 350 degree oven for 20 to 25 minutes.

Makes 10 servings.

Pantry-Quick Fruit Cobbler

Most of these ingredients are found on your pantry shelf.

> 2 cups buttermilk baking mix
> ⅔ cup sugar
> 1 teaspoon cinnamon
> ½ cup melted butter or margarine
> 2 (15-ounce) cans sliced peaches or pears, plums or berries
>   (with juice saved from 1 can)

Mix the buttermilk baking mix, sugar and cinnamon with the melted butter. Pour the peaches and juice in an 8" x 8" baking dish. Sprinkle the butter mixture over the peaches. Bake uncovered in preheated 400 degree oven for 25 minutes, or until golden in color. Serve with vanilla ice cream or non-dairy whipped topping, if desired.

Makes 4 to 6 servings.

Pumpkin-Pecan Crisp

Delightfully different and easily prepared with a cake mix.

1 (12-ounce) can evaporated milk
1 (16-ounce) can pumpkin
3 eggs
1½ cups sugar
4 teaspoons pumpkin pie spice
½ teaspoon salt
1 (18-ounce) package yellow cake mix
1 cup pecans, chopped
½ cup (1 stick) butter, melted, or more if necessary

Butter a 9" x 13" shallow baking dish. In a large bowl, combine evaporated milk, pumpkin, eggs, sugar, pumpkin pie spice and salt; mix well. Pour into baking dish. Sprinkle top of mixture with dry cake mix and smooth gently with fork. Sprinkle top with nuts. Drizzle melted butter over whole pan. If top looks too dry, melt 3 to 4 tablespoons butter and drizzle over dry spots. Bake in preheated 350 degree oven for 55 minutes.

Makes 10 to 12 servings.

Cranberry Crumble

Old or new, this recipe should be on your Thanksgiving menu.

1 (12-ounce) bag cranberries
1 cup sugar
¼ cup orange juice
Grated peel of 1 orange
2 tablespoons orange liqueur
1 cup plus 1 tablespoon flour
½ cup brown sugar
Dash nutmeg
½ teaspoon cinnamon
6 tablespoons cold butter
½ cup chopped walnuts

Rinse cranberries in a colander. In a bowl, combine cranberries with sugar, orange juice, orange peel, liqueur and 1 tablespoon flour. Pour cranberry mixture into a greased, shallow 1½-quart casserole dish.

In a mixing bowl, combine 1 cup flour, brown sugar, nutmeg and cinnamon. Cut butter into small pieces and with fingers or fork, work butter into flour mixture until crumbly. Mix in the walnuts. Sprinkle mixture evenly over cranberries. Bake in preheated 375 degree oven for 40 to 45 minutes or until golden brown and juice begins to run around edges. Serve warm.

Makes 6 to 8 servings.

Banana Chimichangas

The chef at the El Dorado in Santa Fe was gracious enough to share his recipe with us.

6 (6½-inch) square egg roll skins
6 small bananas, peeled
¾ cup milk chocolate chips
Oil for frying (about ½ cup)
Caramel sauce (store bought)
Vanilla, pralines 'n cream or marble fudge ice cream

Lay out egg roll skin on flat surface. Lay banana diagonally on top of egg roll skin, breaking it slightly in middle to straighten it. Sprinkle evenly with 2 tablespoons of chips. Fold in sides of skin and carefully roll up banana. Moisten end flap with water to seal. Repeat with remaining egg roll skins, bananas and chips.

In a skillet large enough to hold three rolls at a time, heat oil until very hot. Fry banana rolls, 3 at a time, until golden on all sides. Drain on paper towels. While still hot, cut 5 slashes in each roll and place each one on plate with a little caramel sauce and a small scoop of ice cream. Drizzle tops with more sauce, if desired.

Makes 6 servings.

Frozen Pistachio Pudding

This molded frozen pudding serves as a dessert — also delicious with dairy, meat or poultry.

1 (3-ounce) package pistachio instant pudding
1 (20-ounce) can crushed pineapple with juice
1 (8-ounce) carton non-dairy whipped topping
4 ounces chopped pistachios, pecans or walnuts, toasted

Put pudding mix in a large bowl. Add crushed pineapple and juice to pudding and stir. Gently fold in whipped topping and add nuts. Spray a 1-quart mold with vegetable spray or line with plastic wrap. Pour mixture into mold. Cover with foil and freeze.

When ready to serve, let pudding stand at room temperature for 15 to 20 minutes. Remove foil. Place serving plate over top and turn upside down. Mold should drop out. If necessary, pull gently on plastic wrap. Smooth out creases with knife.

Makes 8 to 10 servings.

Hint: Use 12-cup mold if recipe is doubled. Allow an additional 15 minutes at room temperature before serving.

Custardy Bread Pudding with Apricots

Our version of a popular dessert served at tea time in a very posh L.A. restaurant.

4 cups cubed egg bread (crust removed; cubes 1½" x 1½")
1 tablespoon melted butter, or butter-flavored spray
2½ cups milk (or part half-and-half)
2 teaspoons vanilla
2 eggs plus 2 egg yolks
⅓ cup sugar
½ cup dried apricots (or pitted prunes), cut into quarters
2 teaspoons grated lemon peel

Put bread cubes on cookie sheet and brush with melted butter or use butter-flavored spray. Bake in preheated 350 degree oven and toast just until golden, not browned. Set aside.

Scald milk; cool for 10 minutes. Add vanilla. Mix eggs, yolks and sugar together in a mixing bowl. Stir in cooled milk.

Combine bread and apricots; put in buttered 1½-quart heatproof loaf pan. Pour liquid mixture over bread. Let pan sit for 10 minutes. Press bread into custard with palm of hand. Sprinkle top with grated lemon peel.

Place loaf pan in larger pan and fill larger pan with enough hot water to come ½ way up the sides of the loaf pan. Bake in 350 degree oven for 55 to 60 minutes or until knife inserted in center comes out clean. Remove from water. Cool for 15 to 20 minutes and then refrigerate for 4 hours before unmolding. Cut into thick slices. Serve with dollop of whipped cream, if desired.

Makes 6 servings.

Chocolate Soufflé

The Beverly Hills Bistro Garden served this soufflé to the "rich and famous" for many years. It was the restaurant's most popular dessert.

> **2 (4-ounce) sweet chocolate baking bars**
> **3 teaspoons powdered instant coffee**
> **5 tablespoons liqueur (orange, chocolate, almond or cherry) or water**
> **½ cup flour**
> **2 cups cold milk (or half-and-half)**
> **½ teaspoon vanilla**
> **5 eggs, separated**
> **2 egg whites**
> **Pinch salt**
> **½ cup sugar**
> **Powdered sugar**
> **Whipped cream, slightly sweetened**

Butter a 2-quart soufflé dish. Encircle top of dish with a buttered 2-inch collar of foil and close with large metal paper clip. In the top of a double boiler, combine chocolate (broken into small pieces), instant coffee and liqueur or water. Stir over moderate heat until mixture is smooth. Set aside and keep warm.

Put flour into a heavy saucepan. Slowly add cold milk, stirring with a whisk until smooth. Set pan over moderate heat and stir constantly until mixture is thick and smooth. Continue to stir for a minute and blend in melted chocolate mixture and vanilla; remove from heat. Beat 5 egg yolks slightly. Stir in a few tablespoons of chocolate and then stir back into chocolate-flour mixture.

Beat egg whites until frothy. Add salt. Continue to beat until soft peaks form. Slowly beat in sugar until stiff peaks form. Stir 2 large spoonfuls of meringue into warm chocolate mixture to lighten. Fold in remaining meringue. At this point, soufflé can stand for 1 hour before baking. Bake in preheated 400 degree oven for 30 to 35 minutes. Sprinkle with powdered sugar and serve with whipped cream, as soon as possible.

Makes 6 to 8 servings.

Frozen Lemon Mousse

If you have a lemon tree, this should be the speciality of your house.

3 eggs, separated
1 cup sugar
3 tablespoons fresh lemon juice
1 tablespoon grated lemon peel
½ teaspoon lemon extract
1 cup whipping cream, whipped, or 3½ cups non-dairy whipped topping,
    partially thawed
Chocolate curls or leaves for garnish, if desired

Beat yolks in electric mixer until thick and light yellow. Beat in sugar, juice, peel and extract. Spoon mixture into top of double boiler. Heat, stirring frequently, for at least 7 to 10 minutes over simmering water. Remove from heat and cool to room temperature.

In bowl of electric mixer, beat egg whites until stiff peaks form. Fold whites into lemon mixture. Whip cream until firm and fold into lemon mixture (or use whipped topping). Freeze in individual serving dishes or in hollowed-out lemon shells until ready to serve. Garnish with chocolate curls or leaves.

Makes 12 servings.

Lemon Meringue Puff (Passover)

This puff is spectacular looking and just as delicious as it looks.

Meringue Puff

> **6 egg whites**
> **¼ teaspoon salt**
> **1½ cups sugar**

Lemon Filling

> **1½ cups sugar**
> **⅓ cup cornstarch**
> **2 cups water**
> **⅓ cup fresh lemon juice**
> **3 egg yolks**
> **1 (12-ounce) carton whipped topping, thawed**

To Make Puff: In bowl of electric mixer, beat egg whites until frothy. Add salt and beat until peaks form. Beat in sugar, 2 tablespoons at a time at low speed. Continue to beat until meringue forms stiff peaks. Heavily grease, with margarine, a deep 10-inch pie pan. Spread a thick layer of meringue over bottom and up sides of pan to form crust. Bake in preheated 300 degree oven for 30 to 45 minutes or until stiff to touch. Turn heat off. Cool in oven for 10 minutes.

To Make Lemon Filling: In a medium-sized saucepan, combine sugar and cornstarch. Whisk in water. Cook over medium heat, stirring constantly until mixture comes to a boil. Boil for 1 minute. Remove from heat. Stir in lemon juice. In a bowl, stir egg yolks with a fork to blend. Add a large spoonful of lemon filling to eggs. Then, slowly stir mixture back into lemon filling in the saucepan. Continue to stir and cook for another minute or two. Remove from heat and pour into a large bowl.

Cover top of filling with plastic wrap. Cool to room temperature. Fold in thawed non-dairy whipped topping. Spoon into meringue shell. Wrap in plastic wrap and freeze. When ready to serve, remove from freezer and thaw in refrigerator for 30 minutes.

Makes 8 to 10 servings.

Sweet Table:

BARS, CANDY & COOKIES

Chocolate Cherry Almond Mandelbread

You'll never believe that these cookies are almost fat-free because they taste so good!

2 cups flour
1 cup raspberry mocha cocoa (may use cocoa powder)
1 teaspoon baking powder
2 extra-large eggs
1 cup sugar
2 teaspoons vanilla
1 cup dried cherries
½ cup chopped toasted almonds
Sugar

In a mixing bowl, combine flour, cocoa and baking powder. In bowl of electric mixer, beat eggs, sugar and vanilla until pale and thick, about 3 minutes. Stir in dry ingredients, then cherries and almonds.

Line a large cookie sheet with foil and spray with oil. With damp hands, shape half the dough into a smooth 12-inch-long log. Place on prepared cookie sheet. Repeat with remaining half of dough. Bake in preheated 350 degree oven for about 20 to 25 minutes. Remove pan from oven and allow to sit for 5 minutes.

Slice logs into 1-inch slices. Lay cookies down on sides. Sprinkle lightly with sugar. Reduce heat to 300 degrees and bake for 10 minutes. Turn cookies on other side and sprinkle with sugar. Return to oven for an additional 5 minutes. Cool on rack.

Makes about 24 cookies.

Hint: For a festive look, melt some chocolate with a few drops of oil and dip one end of cookie into chocolate. Lay on wax paper-lined cookie sheet and refrigerate until chocolate has hardened, about 5 minutes. Store in an airtight container for up to 1 week.

Four-Ingredient Rugelach

If you don't say anything, no one will guess you took a shortcut.

> **2 sticks pie crust mix**
> **1 (3-ounce) package cream cheese (may use ⅓ less fat)**
> **1 tablespoon milk**
> **Raspberry or apricot jam**
> **Powdered sugar or minced walnuts**

In bowl of electric mixer, combine pie crust mix, cream cheese and milk until well blended. Remove mixture from bowl and form into round disc. Cut in half. Refrigerate if dough is too soft or sticky.

Lightly dust flat surface with flour. Roll each disc into a 10-inch square. With pastry wheel (or pizza cutter), cut each square into 16 pieces, each 2½" x 2½". Stir jam and put half teaspoon into center of each. Pinch 2 opposite corners together.

Place dough on greased cookie sheet (or line sheet with foil). Bake in preheated 350 degree oven for 10 to 12 minutes. Remove immediately to wire racks to cool. Sift powdered sugar or finely minced walnuts over tops of rugelach while still warm.

Makes 32 rugelach.

Chocolate Chunk Oatmeal Cookies

Sugar and spice and everything nice!

    ½ cup plus 2 tablespoons butter-flavored shortening or margarine
    I cup firmly packed brown sugar
    I large egg
    2 teaspoons vanilla
    2 teaspoons cinnamon
    1½ cups quick-cooking oats
    I teaspoon baking powder
    1½ cups flour
    1½ cups semisweet chocolate pieces
    ½ cup raisins
    I cup coarsely chopped walnuts (optional)

In large bowl of electric mixer, combine shortening with brown sugar. Beat I minute at medium speed. Scrape sides of bowl. Add egg, vanilla and cinnamon. Beat until mixture is blended well. Reduce speed of mixer to low. Add oats, baking powder and flour; beat until just blended. Stir in chocolate pieces, raisins and nuts.

Fill a small ice cream scoop with dough and press lightly with bottom of hand. Turn dough mounds out on a foil-lined baking sheet, leaving 3 inches between cookies. Bake in preheated 350 degree oven for 12 to 15 minutes. Cool for 2 minutes on baking sheet before removing to wire rack to cool completely.

Makes about 2 dozen cookies.

Chocolate-Dipped Haystacks

Coconut heaven!

> 10 egg whites, slightly beaten
> 2 cups brown sugar
> 7–8 cups flaked coconut
> 1½ cups chopped dates
> 1½ cups chopped walnuts
> ½ teaspoon salt
> 1½ teaspoons vanilla
> 1 cup semisweet chocolate, melted
> ¼ teaspoon oil

Combine egg whites and sugar. Cook over low heat in top of double boiler until mixture reaches 120 degrees on candy thermometer, or feels hot to touch. In a large bowl, combine coconut (start with 7 cups), dates, walnuts, salt and vanilla. Add egg white and sugar mixture and mix well. If too much liquid appears, add more coconut.

Using a small ice cream scoop, form into balls and place on lightly greased baking sheet. Bake in preheated 350 degree oven for 18 to 20 minutes. Cool slightly; then remove from pan to cool thoroughly. Melt 1 cup semisweet chocolate with ¼ teaspoon oil. Dip rounded end of haystack in chocolate.

Makes about 2½ to 3 dozen.

Mazurki (Almond Paste Cookie)

If you like almond paste, you'll love this cookie!

½ **cup sugar**
½ **cup powdered sugar**
3 **tablespoon flour**
3 **large egg whites**
¼ **teaspoon almond extract**
1 **(8-ounce) can almond paste**
⅓ **cup sliced almonds**

In bowl of electric mixer, combine sugar, powdered sugar and flour. Add egg whites, extract and crumbled almond paste. Beat on medium speed until mixture is smooth.

Spoon into a pastry bag with a large star tip (or pack into a cookie press). Press out on greased baking sheet, making rings about 3 inches in diameter (if too thin, make another ring on top). Space about 1 inch apart. Sprinkle rings with almonds. Bake in preheated 350 degree oven until golden, about 12 to 15 minutes. Remove at once from sheet to rack to cool.

Makes approximately 12 to 16 cookies.

Peanut Butter Chocolate Chip Cookies

Kids love this winning combination of flavors in a thick, soft cookie.

2¼ cups flour
1 teaspoon salt
1 teaspoon baking soda
1 stick (½ cup) butter or margarine, at room temperature
½ cup peanut butter (not old-fashioned or chunky)
¾ cup firmly packed brown sugar
¾ cup sugar
1 teaspoon vanilla
2 eggs
2 cups semisweet chocolate chips
1 cup chopped pecans or peanuts

In a small bowl, combine flour, salt and baking soda. Set aside. In a large mixing bowl, beat butter or margarine, peanut butter, both sugars and vanilla until smooth. Add eggs and beat well. Add flour mixture in three parts and mix well. Stir in chocolate chips and pecans.

Drop batter by rounded teaspoonfuls onto ungreased, foil-lined baking sheets. Bake in preheated 375 degree oven for 9 to 11 minutes, depending on size of cookies. Cool for a few minutes on baking sheets before transferring to racks to cool. Store in airtight container. Dough may be frozen.

Makes about 4 dozen cookies.

No-Bake Almond Chocolate Cookies

Not too many cookies are easier to make – or eat!

1 cup semisweet chocolate pieces
1 cup butterscotch pieces
¾ cup sifted powdered sugar
½ cup sour cream (may use light)
1 teaspoon grated lemon peel
¼ teaspoon salt
1¾ cups vanilla wafer crumbs
¾ cup chopped toasted almonds

In microwave-safe bowl, combine chocolate and butterscotch pieces. Heat on high in microwave for 1½ to 2 minutes (can also be melted over hot water). Remove from heat and stir until smooth. Stir in powdered sugar, sour cream, lemon peel and salt until smooth. Blend in wafer crumbs. Refrigerate for 15 to 20 minutes or until firm. Shape into 1-inch balls; then roll in chopped almonds. Store in covered container in refrigerator.

Makes about 3½ dozen cookies.

Chinese Noodle Cookies

Syra Cohn, a resident of the Jewish Home, made these cookies for years to everyone's delight. Now you can too!

1 (12-ounce) package semisweet chocolate chips
1 (12-ounce) package butterscotch chips
1 cup raisins
1 large can Chinese noodles

Combine chips in microwave-safe bowl; heat on high for 3 to 4 minutes or until chips can be blended smoothly. (You can also melt chips in top of double boiler.) Blend in raisins and noodles. Drop by teaspoonfuls onto wax paper-lined cookie sheet. Cool about 1 hour; then refrigerate.

The yield varies, depending on size of cookies.

Lacy Walnut Cups

A beautiful dessert to serve after a special dinner.

6 tablespoons butter or margarine
½ cup brown sugar
4 tablespoons corn syrup
½ cup finely chopped walnuts
⅔ cup flour
½ teaspoon cinnamon
¼ teaspoon salt
Ice cream or sorbet
Fudge sauce
Fresh raspberries or strawberries

Melt butter or margarine; stir in sugar and corn syrup. Add walnuts, flour, cinnamon and salt. Mix well. Drop batter by rounded tablespoonfuls onto a lightly greased baking sheet and smooth with back of spoon to a 3-inch circle. Bake in preheated 375 degree oven for about 8 minutes, or until evenly browned.

Remove from oven and let stand on baking sheet 1 to 1½ minutes, or until edges are firm enough to lift with spatula. Place on inverted custard cups and cool. Repeat with remaining batter. Store in airtight containers. Serve with ice cream or sorbet, fresh fruit and fudge sauce.

Makes 12 cups.

Hint: If you want to make larger cups, use a cereal bowl and make cookies larger to fit.

Almond Hazelnut and Pecan Florentines

These are wonderful for gifts — wrapped first in plastic wrap, then in cellophane and tied with a big ribbon bow.

Florentines

> 2 sticks butter
> 1 cup sugar
> 3 ounces honey
> 3 ounces whipping cream
> 1 pound mixture of sliced natural almonds, hazelnuts and pecans

Chocolate Coating

> 1 cup semisweet chocolate chips
> ½ teaspoon vegetable oil

To Make Florentines: Combine butter, sugar, honey and cream in large, heavy saucepan. Heat over medium heat until mixture boils, stirring frequently. Once mixture boils, cook, stirring constantly, for 1½ minutes. Remove from heat. Stir in mixture of almonds, hazelnuts and pecans.

Divide mixture evenly into six 9-inch greased, aluminum foil pie pans. Spread nut mixture evenly into pans. Bake in preheated 375 degree oven for about 10 to 12 minutes, or until golden brown. Remove from oven and cool. Put in refrigerator for 5 to 10 minutes to harden. Push up on bottom of pan to loosen Florentine. Using a spatula, spread bottom of Florentine with chocolate coating. Let harden in refrigerator. Break into pieces to serve.

To Make Chocolate Coating: Put semisweet chocolate chips and vegetable oil in a small heatproof bowl or use double boiler and heat on high in microwave oven for 1 to 1½ minutes. Stir until smooth.

Makes six 9-inch round Florentines.

Apple Bessie Bars

This is an easy version of an old-time favorite – apple squares – and tastes just as wonderful.

Crust

1 (18-ounce) package "light" yellow cake mix
1 stick softened butter or margarine, sliced into pieces
⅓ cup packed brown sugar
1½ teaspoons cinnamon or apple pie spice

Filling

1 (21-ounce) can apple pie filling
¼ cup packed brown sugar
1 teaspoon cinnamon or apple pie spice
1 tablespoon fresh lemon juice
3 tablespoons oatmeal
½ cup chopped walnuts (optional)

To Make Crust: Mix dry cake mix, butter, brown sugar and cinnamon until crumbly; set aside 1 cup. Press remaining mixture in bottom of a well-greased 8" x 11" x 2" pan.

To Make Filling: In a medium-sized mixing bowl, combine apple pie filling, brown sugar, cinnamon or apple pie spice and lemon juice. Spread evenly over pressed crust. Mix reserved 1 cup crumbs with oatmeal and walnuts, and sprinkle evenly over apple filling. Bake in preheated 350 degree oven for 30 to 35 minutes, or until top is golden brown. Cool 10 minutes. Run sharp knife around edges to loosen. Let cool for at least 20 minutes before cutting into bars.

Makes 12 bars.

Almost Fat-Free Fudgy Brownies

A very popular treat when you're watching your fat intake.

> **2 egg whites (about ¼ cup)**
> **2 teaspoons canola oil**
> **2 teaspoons vanilla**
> **2 tablespoons corn syrup**
> **¼ cup plus 2 tablespoons unsweetened applesauce**
> **½ cup plus 2 tablespoons sugar**
> **½ cup dark brown sugar, packed**
> **⅔ cup flour**
> **½ cup plus 3 tablespoons unsweetened cocoa**
> **½ teaspoon baking powder**

In bowl of food processor, put egg whites, oil, vanilla, corn syrup and applesauce; turn motor on until blended. Add both sugars, turn motor on and mix. Combine flour, cocoa and baking powder. Add to food processor and turn motor on and off until smooth.

Pour mixture into 8" x 8" baking pan that has been sprayed with vegetable oil or butter-flavored spray. Bake in preheated 350 degree oven for 18 minutes. Do not overbake. Cool and cut into 2-inch squares. Sprinkle top with powdered sugar.

Makes 16 squares.

Stacey's Almond Roca

Nothing beats "homemade!"

2 sticks butter
1 cup sugar
1 tablespoon water
12 (1-ounce) chocolate bars or 12 ounces semisweet chocolate chips
5 ounces slivered almonds, chopped and lightly toasted

Melt butter in heavy skillet. Stir in sugar and water, stirring constantly over medium heat. Cook until mixture is the color of peanut butter. Quickly pour mixture into well-greased, foil-lined 9" x 9" square pan. Let mixture harden.

Lay 6 of the chocolate bars (or half the chocolate chips) on top of toffee, side by side. Spread chocolate as it melts and press half of the almonds lightly into chocolate. Turn pan over onto foil-lined cookie sheet. Remove foil from top of toffee. Repeat chocolate and almond procedure. Cool until chocolate is firm. Cut into bite-sized pieces.

Makes about 36 pieces.

Wolfgang Puck's Apricot Macaroons (Passover)

Unbelievably delicious — especially if you love apricots.

½ **cup dried apricots, cut into quarters**
½ **cup water**
¾ **cup plus 1 tablespoon sugar**
4 egg whites
4½ **cups unsweetened shredded coconut**

In a small saucepan, combine apricots, water and 1 tablespoon sugar. Cook apricots over medium heat until tender and about 1 tablespoon water remains. Cool slightly and transfer to a food processor fitted with a steel blade. Add remaining sugar, egg whites and ½ cup coconut. Process by first using on-off spurts, and then allow machine to run until apricots are pureed. Transfer to large bowl of electric mixer. Add remaining coconut. Beat on medium speed until coconut is well blended. Stop machine and check the texture. Mixture should hold together when pinched. Continue to mix, if necessary.

Using your hands, shape mixture into pointed cone shapes. Arrange 1 inch apart on parchment paper or foil on cookie sheets. Bake in preheated 350 degree oven for 15 to 20 minutes until the tops are well browned. Cool on rack. Store in airtight container.

Makes 24 to 32 macaroons.

Double Chocolate Macaroons (Passover)

Pretty enough for any pastry tray.

Macaroons

> 1½ cups blanched almonds, finely ground
> 1½ cups powdered sugar
> 3 egg whites

Chocolate Frosting

> 4 tablespoons butter or margarine, softened
> 3–3½ cups powdered sugar
> ½ cup semisweet chocolate pieces, melted
> 3 egg yolks
> ¼ teaspoon almond extract

Chocolate Glaze

> 6 ounces semisweet chocolate
> 1 tablespoon shortening

To Make Macaroons: Whirl nuts in food processor, using steel blade, until finely ground. Add powdered sugar and whirl just to blend. Set aside. Beat egg whites until foamy. Continue beating until stiff peaks form. Sprinkle nut mixture over egg whites ⅓ at a time, folding together until blended. Drop rounded teaspoonfuls of the mixture about 1 inch apart on baking sheets lined with brown wrapping paper. Bake in preheated 350 degree oven until lightly browned, about 15 minutes. Let cool for about 5 minutes; then use a wide spatula to remove from pan. Cool. Spread with Chocolate Frosting and top with Chocolate Glaze.

To Make Chocolate Frosting: Combine all ingredients in a mixer bowl. Mix until creamy smooth. Spread frosting generously over bottom of each cooled cookie. Place cookies frosting side up on cookie sheet and refrigerate for 15 minutes.

To Make Chocolate Glaze: Melt chocolate and shortening in top of double boiler. Remove from heat and stir to cool. When lukewarm, dip unfrosted side of cookie in glaze to coat. Chill again for at least 10 minutes. Store in refrigerator for up to 3 days, or cookies can be frozen. Defrost in refrigerator for at least 3 hours before serving.

Makes about 4 dozen.

Cinnamon-Nut Mandelbread (Passover)

These are so delicious, you better hide them or you won't have any for company!

6 large eggs
1½ cups sugar
1½ cups oil
1 cup chopped almonds or hazelnuts
1 cup matzo meal
1 cup matzo cake meal
1 tablespoon potato flour
1 tablespoon cinnamon
Juice of 1 small lemon (2 tablespoons)
Cinnamon-sugar topping (1 tablespoons cinnamon and 4 tablespoons sugar)

Mix all ingredients in the order listed, except the cinnamon-sugar topping, and refrigerate for 2 to 4 hours until dough thickens. On a cookie sheet, place two 6" x 14" heavy aluminum foil sheets. Fold up 1 inch on all sides, pinching corners together to form 2 baking tins. Lightly grease the bottom of each foil "tin." Fill each "tin" with half the batter. Bake in preheated 350 degree oven for 30 minutes or until cake tester comes out clean. Remove mandelbread from foil. Cut into ½-inch slices and dip each side of slice into the cinnamon-sugar mixture. Return to cookie sheet and bake on each side an additional 10 minutes to brown.

Makes about 5 dozen.

Walnut and Chocolate Chip Mandelbread (Passover)

You won't believe these are made with matzo cake meal.

    2 cups sugar
    ½ pound margarine or butter
    6 eggs
    2¾ cups cake meal
    ¾ cup potato starch
    ½ teaspoon salt
    1 teaspoon cinnamon
    1 (12-ounce) package chocolate chips
    ¼ cup chopped nuts (walnuts, pecans, almonds)

In a medium-sized mixing bowl, cream together sugar and margarine. Add eggs, one at a time, beating well after each egg. In a large mixing bowl, sift together cake meal, potato starch, salt and cinnamon. Fold in egg mixture. Stir in chocolate chips and nuts.

Form dough into 2-inch-wide loaves and place on a greased cookie sheet. Bake in preheated 350 degree oven for 30 to 45 minutes or until golden brown. After cooling slightly, cut into slices. At this point, the mandelbread may be put back into the oven for 5 minutes for a browner cookie.

Makes about 8 dozen.

Gerschmirte Matzo (Passover)

Very different and very good!

> ½ cup milk
> 4 matzos
> 1 (16-ounce) package soft cream cheese
> ½ cup sour cream
> ½ cup sugar
> 1 tablespoon potato starch
> Juice of ½ lemon
> 3 eggs
> 1 tablespoon cinnamon-sugar mixture

Pour milk into a large shallow dish and lay matzos in one at a time, turning to soak both sides. Set matzos on a greased foil-lined baking sheet. Beat remaining ingredients, except cinnamon-sugar mixture, until smooth. Spoon onto matzos, spreading to cover. Sprinkle with cinnamon-sugar mixture. Bake in preheated 350 degree oven for 10 to 15 minutes until puffed and lightly browned. Remove from oven immediately and cut each matzo into squares.

Makes 36 squares.

Chocolate Chip Cookies (Passover)

A delicate crisp cookie that is addictive!

> **1½ cups brown sugar, firmly packed**
> **½ cup granulated sugar**
> **2 tablespoons Passover vanilla sugar or 1 teaspoon imitation vanilla**
> **1 cup unsalted butter or margarine**
> **2 eggs**
> **¼ teaspoon salt (optional)**
> **½ cup matzo meal**
> **½ cup matzo cake meal**
> **1 cup potato starch**
> **2 cups chocolate chips**

Cream both sugars together with vanilla sugar and butter or margarine. Blend in eggs. Stir in salt, matzo meal, cake meal, potato starch and chocolate chips. Chill dough for an hour or overnight. (The dough may be frozen before baking.)

Line several baking sheets with parchment paper or foil. Scoop dough by teaspoonfuls onto baking sheet, leaving room for spreading. Bake in preheated 350 degree oven for 12 minutes. Let cookies sit on baking parchment for 10 to 15 minutes, until just cool. Using a metal spatula, transfer cookies to cooling racks for complete cooling.

Makes about 9 dozen cookies.

Hint: You can add spices or chopped nuts, if you like. And yes, this recipe really calls for one cup of potato starch.

Jam Slices (Passover)

One of the quickest cookies to make – with the best results.

> 1½ **cups nuts (walnuts, almonds or hazelnuts), finely chopped in blender or food processor**
> ⅓ **cup sugar**
> 1–2 **egg whites, unbeaten**
> 1½ **cups thick jam**

Grease a baking sheet. In bowl of electric mixer, combine nuts with sugar. Add egg whites a little at a time to bind mixture. Form into a long roll 1½ inches in diameter. Gently place on baking sheet. Make a deep ridge with the side of your hand the length of the roll. Bake in preheated 350 degree oven for 15 to 20 minutes until light brown. Meanwhile, heat jam in a small saucepan until boiling. Fill ridge of nut roll with jam immediately when taking baking sheet from oven. Cool. Cut into diagonal slices.

Mocha Pecan Brownies (Passover)

You can even indulge yourself during Passover with these cookies.

> ¾ **cup peanut oil**
> 2 **cups sugar**
> 4 **eggs**
> ½ **cup cocoa**
> 1 **cup matzo cake meal**
> 2 **tablespoons potato starch**
> ½ **cup black coffee**
> 1 **cup chopped pecans or walnuts**

In a large mixing bowl, cream oil and sugar until light and fluffy. Beat in eggs, one at a time, beating well after each addition. In a small bowl, combine cocoa, cake meal and potato starch; add to oil mixture, alternating with coffee. Fold in nuts. Pour batter into a well-greased 8-inch square pan and bake in preheated 350 degree oven for 1 hour, or until toothpick inserted into center comes out clean. Cool; then cut into squares.

Makes 16 squares.

English Toffee Bars (Passover)

You will not believe how unbelievable these cookies are!

>   3 pieces matzo
>   1 cup (2 sticks) butter
>   1 cup brown sugar
>   1 (12-ounce) package chocolate chips
>   1 cup finely chopped nuts (walnuts, peanuts)

Line a cookie sheet with foil. Butter foil. Lay matzos on cookie sheet in 1 layer, side by side. Melt butter; add brown sugar and boil for 5 minutes. Watch carefully. Pour melted mixture on matzos and spread evenly. Bake in preheated 325 degree oven for 8 to 10 minutes. Turn off oven; sprinkle on chocolate chips and put back in oven to melt chips, about 8 minutes. Take cookie sheet out of oven, and spread chips across evenly; sprinkle on nuts and press lightly into chocolate. Refrigerate for 1 hour. Break into pieces. Store in refrigerator.

Chocolate Walnut Candy (Passover)

Super easy – super good!

>   1 (12-ounce) package semisweet chocolate chips
>   ½ teaspoon oil
>   1 cup matzo farfel
>   1 cup coarsely chopped walnuts or raisins

Melt chocolate chips and oil in microwave in a medium-sized bowl on high, about 2 minutes. Stir until mixture is smooth. Mix in farfel and nuts. Drop by teaspoonfuls onto a wax paper-lined cookie sheet. Put into refrigerator to harden until ready to serve. Freeze if not serving immediately.

Makes approximately 40 pieces.

Farfel Nut Florentine (Passover)

Unusual and delicious!

> 1 cup matzo farfel
> 1 tablespoon matzo cake meal
> 1 cup sugar
> ¼ teaspoon salt
> ½ cup melted unsalted margarine
> 1 egg, beaten
> 1 teaspoon vanilla or 1 tablespoon orange juice
> ½ cup finely chopped almonds
> ¼ cup sliced almonds

Line a baking pan with foil or parchment paper. If using foil, be sure to have the shiny side up. In a medium bowl, combine matzo farfel, cake meal, sugar and salt; mix well. Pour margarine over mixture and blend until sugar dissolves. Add the egg and vanilla or orange juice; blend. Mix in the almonds. Drop the farfel mixture by teaspoonfuls onto the lined pan, about 2 inches apart. Allow sufficient space as the mixture will spread. Bake in preheated 325 degree oven for 8 to 10 minutes or until golden brown.

Slip foil off of baking sheet and allow to cool on counter while preparing the next batch. Peel foil away; do not use spatula. You might want to carefully tear or cut the foil around each cookie and then peel foil slowly off. It takes a bit of practice, but the result is worth it!

Makes about 2 dozen cookies.

I Remember Mama:

RECIPES FROM THE PAST

"The Real Thing" Chopped Liver

"We all love this recipe and you will too!"   ***Tova Weltman***

> 1½ pounds calves or chicken livers (or half of each)
> 4–6 tablespoons chicken fat (may use part oil)
> 2–3 medium onions, chopped
> 4 hard-cooked eggs
> 1½ teaspoons salt, or to taste
> ¼ teaspoon pepper, or to taste

Rinse liver and pat dry with a paper towel. Heat 4 tablespoons of chicken fat or oil in a large skillet over moderate heat. Add onions and sauté until onions are golden brown, stirring frequently. Remove to plate to cool. If needed, add more fat to the pan and heat. Lay slices of liver or chicken livers in pan not touching. Sauté for about 8 to 10 minutes, browning both sides. Remove from pan. Cool to room temperature. Cut liver into pieces. Spoon any liquid left in pan over liver.

Instead of chicken fat or oil, the onions and livers can be sautéed in ½ cup chicken stock to reduce fat content. Use a large skillet and cook over moderate heat until onions are tender and liver has lost any pink color.

Grinder Method: Put all prepared ingredients through a grinder, then into a bowl. Add salt and pepper to taste. You may need a little chicken fat. Stir until all ingredients are blended. Refrigerate.

Food Processor Method: Put ⅓ of the onions and ⅓ of the liver into bowl of food processor, using steel blade. Turn motor on and off in spurts until mixture is of desired consistency. Repeat process with remaining onions and liver. Grate eggs and add to liver mixture in a large bowl. Season with salt and pepper. Stir until all ingredients are blended. Refrigerate until serving.

Makes 2 to 2½ pounds.

Hint: *The secret in getting the same texture as in the grinder method is to turn the food processor on and off in spurts. Grate the eggs to create more texture.*

Betty's Best Brisket Knishes

"Mom never had it this easy – frozen puff pastry and a food processor take all the hard work out of making knishes." **Sherry Watnick**

1 pound leftover well-seasoned, roasted brisket or tri-tip, cut into 1" x 2" pieces
1 medium onion, finely chopped and sautéed in 1 tablespoon oil until browned
1 egg, beaten
Salt and ground pepper to taste
1 frozen puff pastry sheet (from a 17-ounce package of 2 sheets)
Egg wash (1 egg beaten with 2 teaspoons water)
Sesame seeds (optional)

In bowl of food processor, evenly distribute pieces of meat in one layer. Turn motor on and off until meat is finely chopped. Repeat until all meat is used. In a mixing bowl, combine meat, browned onions, beaten egg, and salt and pepper to taste. Set aside.

When ready to use, divide meat into thirds. On a flat surface, form each third into rope the size of the pastry (about 14 inches long). Thaw a frozen sheet of puff pastry until it can be rolled out, about 10 to 15 inches. Lightly flour a flat surface (a marble slab is very good). Roll sheet to a 15" x 9" rectangle. Cut a 9-inch side into 3 strips, each 3 inches wide (3" x 15"). Carefully place each meat roll along one 15-inch edge of pastry strip. Roll the pastry over the meat and seal the edges with egg wash. Using side of hand as a knife, cut rolls into 1½-inch slices. Press and flatten one side, which will be the bottom. Twist cut side on top and push slightly into center "like a belly button." Chill for 1 hour. Place on foil-lined cookie sheets (ungreased). Brush with egg wash. Sprinkle with sesame seeds, if desired. Bake for 12 minutes or until pastry is puffed and golden.

Makes approximately 30 knishes.

Cecelia's Gefilte Fish from Scratch

"If there is ever a day you want to make gefilte fish from scratch, this is the recipe you want to use."
Harriet Part

Fish Stock

> **Bones from fish**
> **2–3 medium onions, sliced**
> **2–3 carrots, sliced**
> **6 cups water**
> **1 tablespoon salt**
> **1 teaspoon pepper**
> **½ tablespoon sugar**

Fish

> **4 pounds fish fillets (whitefish, pike, cod), cut into pieces, save bones**
> **1 medium onion, quartered**
> **4 eggs, beaten**
> **4 teaspoons salt, or to taste**
> **1½ teaspoons white pepper**
> **1 teaspoon sugar**
> **3–4 tablespoons matzo meal**
> **½ cup water, if necessary**

To Make Fish Stock: Place fish bones in a 6-quart stockpot. Add remaining ingredients and bring to a boil. Remove any scum that surfaces. Turn heat lower so that stock barely boils. Simmer, covered for 30 minutes. Remove bones, onions and carrots from stock, which is now ready to be used as poaching liquid for fish.

To Make Fish: Grind fish and onion in batches until finely chopped in food processor or food grinder. Place mixture in a large bowl and beat in remaining ingredients. Shape fish into balls or ovals with wet hands. Carefully drop fish into stock. Cover and cook over low heat for 1½ hours. Stir frequently. Remove fish carefully. Chill with some of the poaching liquid.

Makes 12 to 16 pieces.

Mama's Swedish Meatballs

Based on an original recipe for Köttbullar sent to us from a friend in Minnesota. "It's wonderful!"
Thelma Rifkind

½ **cup soft bread crumbs**
1 **cup non-dairy creamer**
½ **pound twice ground beef**
½ **pound ground veal**
1 **egg**
1 **teaspoon salt**
¼ **teaspoon seasoned pepper**
¼ **teaspoon each nutmeg and ginger**
2 **tablespoons margarine**
½ **cup finely minced onion**
2–3 **tablespoons oil**
Flour
⅓ **cup non-dairy creamer**
⅓ **cup beef stock**

Combine bread crumbs and ½ cup non-dairy creamer in a large mixing bowl for 10 to 15 minutes. Add beef and veal, egg, salt, pepper, nutmeg and ginger. Set aside. In a small frying pan, heat margarine until bubbly and sauté onions until tender. Add to beef mixture and beat while adding remaining ½ cup non-dairy creamer. Refrigerate for 1 hour or until meat is firm enough to handle. Roll into appetizer-size meatballs.

Put oil in a large skillet over medium heat. Add meatballs, but do not crowd pan. Sauté until cooked through and browned on all sides. Remove with a slotted spoon and drain. Sprinkle meatballs lightly with flour. To same pan, stir in creamer and stock over low heat. Add meatballs, continuing to stir and cook until sauce thickens slightly. Taste for seasoning.

Makes 6 to 8 servings.

"Bread Machine" Challah

No "knead" to worry about this recipe. It tastes as good as it looks on the cover of the cookbook.

      1 package active dry yeast
      1¼ cups warm water (about 110 degrees)
      1 teaspoon salt
      ¾ cup sugar
      ¼ cup salad oil
      2 eggs, slightly beaten
      2 or 3 drops yellow food coloring or pinch of saffron
      5–5½ cups flour, unsifted
      1 egg yolk, beaten with 1 tablespoon water
      1 tablespoon sesame seeds or poppy seeds

Place yeast and warm water in bread machine pan, following your machine's instructions. After the yeast has started bubbling, add the remaining ingredients except the egg yolk and sesame seeds. Follow instructions for your bread machine in the manual mode.

When the bread machine signals completion of the rising cycle, turn the dough out onto a lightly floured board. Punch the dough down and knead briefly to release any captured air. Set aside and cover ¾ cup dough.

Divide remaining dough into 4 equal portions; roll each between hands to form a strand about 20 inches long. Place the 4 strips lengthwise on a greased baking sheet, pinch tops together and braid as follows: Pick up strand on right, bring it over next one, under the third and over the fourth. Repeat, always starting with strand on right, until braid is complete. Pinch ends together.

Roll reserved dough into a strip about 15 inches long; cut into 3 strips and make a small 3-strand braid. Lay on top center of large braid. Cover and let rise in a warm place until almost doubled, about 1 hour.

Using a soft brush or your fingers, spread egg yolk mixture evenly over braids; sprinkle with seeds. Bake in a preheated 350 degree oven for 30 to 35 minutes or until loaf is golden brown and sounds hollow when tapped. Serve warm, or let cool on rack.

Makes 1 loaf.

Crunchy Onion Poppyseed Biscuits

"These biscuits are sometimes called proschekes. That's the name my mother always called them. The more you chew them, the better they are." **Anne Goldstein**

> 4 cups flour
> 1 ⅛ teaspoons salt
> Dash white pepper
> 2 ½ teaspoons baking powder
> 1 tablespoon sugar
> 1 medium onion, diced
> 1 ½ ounces poppy seeds
> 1 cup oil
> 1 egg, beaten
> ½ cup warm water

In a large mixing bowl, stir flour, salt, white pepper, baking powder and sugar together. Make a well in center of flour mixture. Add onions, poppy seeds, oil, egg and warm water. Stir with a fork until mixture starts to come together to form a dough.

Flour hands lightly. Use hands to form dough into a ball. Divide in half. Roll dough on lightly floured board to about ¾ inch thickness. Cut into squares about 3" x 3". Repeat with remaining dough. Place on foil-lined cookie sheets. Bake in preheated 375 degree oven for about 45 to 55 minutes or until golden brown. This biscuit is very crunchy and not like an American biscuit.

Makes about 36.

Cheese Blintzes

"Everyone loves cheese blintzes! The secret to this recipe is keeping the 'bletlach' (crêpes) thin, thin, thin."
Thelma Rifkind

Filling

1½ pounds farmer's cheese
1 egg (do not use egg substitute)
1 teaspoon lemon flavoring
2–4 tablespoons sugar
1 teaspoon cinnamon

Crêpe Batter

3–4 eggs (do not use egg substitute)
1½ cups milk
1½ cups flour
¼ teaspoon baking powder
2 tablespoons melted butter or margarine
4 tablespoons margarine, melted (may need more)
2 wet kitchen towels (wrung out well), placed on counter

To Make Filling: In a medium (non-metal) bowl, mix together all ingredients for filling. Cover and place in refrigerator.

To Make Crêpe Batter: For crêpe batter, mix together eggs and milk; place in a food processor. Add flour and baking powder, a little at a time (batter should be like thin mayonnaise). Add 2 tablespoons melted butter.

Heat a 9-inch non-stick frying pan until hot (water will sizzle when sprinkled on pan). Dip a pastry brush into melted margarine and brush the pan with a thin coat. Heat again (not to smoking stage). Pour a small amount of batter (about ¼ cup) into the pan and swirl around until covered; empty any excess batter back into remaining batter. Heat until sides pull away (if edge of batter sticks to sides of pan, gently pull away with a knife). Turn crêpe out onto a damp dish towel and return pan to stove to heat again. Brush margarine in pan and swirl another ¼ cup of batter and pour off excess. Repeat with remaining batter. Slightly overlap crêpes on towels to cool.

To Assemble Blintze: Place 1 tablespoon of filling on one edge of crêpe; roll forward twice, then fold both sides and continue rolling to end. (Blintzes can be frozen at this point.) Fry blintzes, both sides, in butter until golden brown. Serve with one or all of the following: sour cream, applesauce, cinnamon, fresh or frozen strawberries, jam, honey or syrup.

Makes 15 to 20 cheese-filled blintzes depending on thickness of crêpe.

Variation: May substitute fruit pie filling for cheese filling recipe above, or use some of each.

Lower-Fat Crêpe Batter

"For a different type of crêpe that is lower in fat, try this one. My mother made this unusual batter with cornstarch instead of flour, and it is very thin."   ***Bobbi Delevie***

Crêpe Batter

> **4 eggs, well beaten**
> **1 cup cornstarch**
> **½ teaspoon salt**
> **1 cup water**

Beat ingredients together and follow directions for previous recipe.

Kreplach with Onion and Mushroom Filling

"My mother, Blanche Segal, handed down the original recipe to me from my grandmother – and so it will go from generation to generation."   **Claire Kunin**

Dough

> 1¾ cups flour
> ½ teaspoon salt
> 2 eggs
> 1½ tablespoons water

Filling

> 2 tablespoons oil
> 8 ounces mushrooms, chopped
> 1 cup finely chopped onions
> 1 small clove garlic, minced
> 1 tablespoon minced parsley
> 1 teaspoon minced fresh dill
> Bread crumbs
> Salt and pepper to taste

To Make Dough: In a large mixing bowl, mix flour and salt. Make a well in the center and put eggs and water in it. With a fork, work in the flour until a dough is formed. Remove from bowl to a lightly floured board and knead until smooth and elastic. Roll out as thin as possible. Cut into 3-inch squares. Put 1 tablespoon of Onion-Mushroom Filling on each square. Fold dough over the filling to form a triangle. Press edges together firmly. Drop into simmering water or chicken stock. Cook over moderate heat for 15 to 20 minutes.

To Make Onion-Mushroom Filling: Heat oil in a large skillet. Add mushrooms, onions, garlic, parsley and dill; sauté for 10 minutes or until any mushroom liquid has evaporated. Add enough bread crumbs to bind mixture together. Season to taste with salt and pepper.

Makes about 18 kreplach.

Hint: Won ton skins can be used in place of kreplach dough – a very easy alternative. Brisket filling from Betty's Best Brisket Knishes can also be used to fill the kreplach.

"Depression Days" Potato Soup

This soup was popular during the Depression, and it can lift your spirits even now.

4 tablespoons unsalted butter
1 medium onion, chopped
3½ tablespoons flour
4 cups water
1½ teaspoons salt
½ teaspoon garlic salt
1 teaspoon dried dill or 1 tablespoon snipped fresh dill
½ teaspoon seasoned pepper
3 large russet potatoes, peeled and diced
2 tablespoons finely minced parsley

In a 6-quart pot, melt butter over moderate heat until it turns brown (but not burnt). Add onions and cook, stirring constantly for a few minutes. Be careful not to burn onions. Blend in flour; remove pot from heat; whisk in water and return to heat. Add seasonings and potatoes. Bring soup to a boil, stirring occasionally. Lower heat; add parsley and dill. Cover pot and simmer for 25 to 30 minutes. Taste for seasonings.

Makes 3 to 4 servings.

Poet Shelley's Chicken Soup

"My husband and I were 'engaged to be engaged,' but when I made this soup for dinner, he proposed that night!" **Shelley Greenspan**, *a resident at the Jewish Home*

1 pound chicken wings
1 ½ pounds cut-up chicken parts
3 carrots, sliced
3 celery stalks (with leaves), cut into pieces
2 parsnips, cut into pieces
2 tablespoons parsley leaves
¾ teaspoon dried dill
2 medium onions, cut into quarters (leave on peel)
8 cups water
1 tablespoon salt
White pepper to taste

Combine all ingredients, except salt and pepper, in a large 6-quart stockpot. Bring to a boil. Skim foam off the top. Cover and cook over medium heat for 2 hours or until chicken is tender. Season with salt and pepper to taste. Strain the soup and serve with any desired soup garnish, such as matzo balls, noodles or rice.

Makes 6 servings.

Chicken in the Pot

Once you've made the chicken soup and matzo balls, the rest is easy. And what could be better on a cold winter evening!

6 cups clear homemade chicken soup
2–3 fresh carrots, cut into chunks
2 celery stalks, sliced
1 cup frozen peas
4 wings (previously cooked in soup)

4 legs or thighs (previously cooked in soup)
2 tablespoons minced parsley
2 large or 4 medium matzo balls (kept warm)

In a large 6-quart stockpot, put previously made chicken soup that has been strained of all chicken and vegetables. About 15 to 20 minutes before serving, add fresh carrots, celery and frozen peas to soup. Simmer until carrots are tender. During the last 10 minutes, add chicken parts to reheat thoroughly. When ready to serve, ladle soup and chicken into soup tureen or large soup bowls. Add vegetables, minced parsley and matzo balls.

Makes 4 servings.

My Mother's Matzo Balls

"If you like them 'light,' this is the recipe; if you like them 'heavy,' add more matzo meal."   **Ruth Nussbaum**

4 tablespoons vegetable shortening, melted
4 eggs
1 cup matzo meal, or more
1–2 tablespoons soda water
1 tablespoon rendered chicken fat (optional)
Salt and pepper to taste

Put melted vegetable shortening in a medium bowl. Stir in one egg after another. Add matzo meal and mix well. Add remaining ingredients. Refrigerate mixture for 25 minutes.

Form marble-sized matzo balls. Cook in boiling, slightly salted water or chicken stock (made with mix or cubes) for 10 to 15 minutes covered, or until balls rise to the top and have almost doubled in size. Matzo balls can be frozen.

Makes approximately 35 balls.

I Remember Mama

Sweet-and-Sour Cabbage Soup with Sauerkraut

"A wonderful Old World soup that is as good today as it was years ago."   ***Pearl Rosen***

1½ pounds flanken, chuck or short ribs
2 beef bones
1 tablespoon oil
1 small cabbage, coarsely shredded
1 (28-ounce) can whole tomatoes
2 medium onions, chopped
8 cups beef stock (or 8 cups water and 8 bouillon cubes)
2 cloves garlic, minced
Sour salt or lemon juice to taste (¼ cup lemon juice)
Brown sugar to taste (about ¼ to 1 cup)
1 (16-ounce) can sauerkraut
Salt to taste
Ground black pepper to taste

Cut meat into pieces; brown in hot oil in a 6-quart stockpot. Add bones and brown. Stir in cabbage, tomatoes, onions and beef stock. Bring to a boil. Skim the top. Cover and cook over medium heat for 2 hours. Add garlic, sour salt (or lemon juice), sugar and sauerkraut; cook 30 minutes longer. Season to taste with salt and pepper. Taste and adjust for sweet-and-sour.

Makes 6 servings.

Mushroom Barley and Beef Soup

"This hearty soup is a meal in itself and just the aroma is nostalgic…. My mother used to tell me stories of how she would pick the mushrooms for her mother when she was a girl in Austria." **Harriet Part**

I pound beef short ribs
I tablespoon oil
2 medium onions, chopped
2 cloves garlic, minced
2 large carrots, sliced
2 stalks celery, sliced
½ cup medium barley, washed and drained
¼ cup dried lima beans
10 dried mushrooms, rinsed and soaked in I cup hot water (save water)
8½ cups beef stock
2–3 teaspoons salt
½ teaspoon pepper
I cup sliced fresh mushrooms (optional)

Brown meat on all sides in hot oil in a large 6-quart stockpot. Add onions, garlic, carrots and celery; sauté for 10 minutes, stirring often. Add barley, lima beans, dried mushrooms, water from mushrooms and beef stock. Bring to a boil. Skim any foam that rises to the top. Turn heat lower; add salt and pepper. Cover pot and cook 2½ hours. Fresh mushrooms may be added the last 20 minutes of cooking. Taste for seasonings. Cool before refrigerating. When soup is completely chilled, fat may be removed from top. Soup can be frozen.

Makes 4 to 5 servings.

Vegetarian Split Pea Soup

"My mother made this soup and we all loved it then – and my family loves it now."   **Bobbi Delevie**

2 quarts water
2 cups green split peas
3 stalks celery, coarsely chopped
2–3 large carrots, chopped
2 medium onions, chopped
1½–2 teaspoons ground thyme
Pinch cayenne
2 bay leaves
Salt and pepper to taste (start with 1 tablespoon salt)

Combine all ingredients in a 6-quart stockpot. Boil hard for 20 minutes. Lower heat and simmer until peas are tender (45 to 60 minutes). Strain through a fine sieve, if desired, or puree in a food processor (but first remove bay leaves). Return to pot and bring to boiling point.

Makes 6 to 8 servings.

Tomato Rice Soup

"I think Campbell's got the idea for this soup from my grandmother Minnie – she made it for years."
Gloria Getzug

> 1 pound flanken
> 3 stalks celery with tops, cut into large pieces
> 3–4 carrots, cut into large pieces
> 1 medium onion, chopped
> 1 (46-ounce) can tomato juice and equal amount of beef stock
> 1 teaspoon thyme
> 2–3 teaspoons salt
> ½ teaspoon pepper
> ½ cup rice

Put flanken, celery, carrots, onion, tomato juice and beef stock in a 3½- to 4-quart stockpot. Bring to a boil. Skim any foam that rises to the top. Add thyme, salt and pepper. Cover and simmer for 2 to 2½ hours, or until meat is tender. Add rice the last ½ hour. Remove onion and celery.

Makes 8 to 10 servings.

Kosher Dill Pickles

"This started out as a 'shitarine' recipe, but after many tries we came up with a recipe with measurements that work." **Ilse Diament**

  18 small, firm cucumbers
  1 bunch dill
  6–8 cloves garlic, peeled
  Water (enough to fill jars – measure before starting recipe)
  3 tablespoons salt
  1 tablespoon pickling spice
  2 tablespoons white vinegar
  2–3 bay leaves

Have enough jars to hold cucumbers packed closely together. Sterilize jars in dishwasher along with lids. Wash cucumbers thoroughly. Put a few sprigs of dill in bottom of jars. Add garlic cloves, then layer of cucumbers, then dill and garlic; end with cucumbers and dill on top.

Mix water with salt, pickling spice and vinegar. Add bay leaf to each jar. Pour vinegar mixture into jars until filled to top. Leave jars opened but covered with layer of cheesecloth or paper towel until cucumbers change color. This should take 7 to 10 days. Jars can then be closed and refrigerated.

Makes 18 pickles.

Cabbage and Beef Borscht

"My son had me teach the cook at his deli how to make this soup, and, if I say so myself, it is delicious."
Mollie Gornbein, *a resident at the Jewish Home*

1½ pounds short ribs
2 pounds cabbage, shredded
1 large onion, finely chopped
3 carrots, sliced
1 (8-ounce) can tomato sauce
7 cups water (add beef bouillon cubes for richer stock)
½ pound fresh mushrooms, sliced
2–3 teaspoons salt, or more to taste
½ teaspoon pepper, or more to taste

Heat stockpot until drop of water sizzles. Add short ribs and bones, turning as meat browns on all sides. Add cabbage, onion and carrots. Cook for a few minutes longer. Add tomato sauce and water (or beef stock). Cook until meat is tender, about 1½ to 2 hours. Add mushrooms, salt and pepper; continue cooking for 15 to 20 minutes.

Makes 4 to 6 servings.

Stuffed Cabbage My Way

"This is an old family favorite of my mother, Lillian Ross. The recipe is long on reading but is very easy to make and delicious to eat."   **Barbara Bernstein**

Stuffed Cabbage

> 3 pounds lean ground beef or turkey
> 2 teaspoons salt
> ¾ teaspoon pepper
> 1 teaspoon celery salt
> ½ cup ketchup
> 2 eggs or egg substitute
> ½ cup crushed unsalted crackers
> 2 large heads green cabbage
> 3 cups chopped onions

Sauce

> 2 (12-ounce) bottles chili sauce
> 1 (12-ounce) jar grape jelly

To Make Stuffed Cabbage: In a large bowl, combine meat, salt, pepper, celery salt, ketchup, eggs and crushed crackers. Mix with hands just until mixture is well combined. Set aside.

Cut out and discard hard center core of each cabbage. Place in 3 inches of boiling water in the bottom of a large kettle. Steam cabbages one at a time until leaves are flexible and can be removed easily from the head, about 5 minutes. If necessary, return cabbage to hot water to soften inner leaves.

Using a ¼-cup measure, scoop meat mixture into hands and form into a 3" x 1" roll, making 28 rolls. Place each meat roll on a drained cabbage leaf and fold top of leaf over meat; then fold sides and roll up into an oblong shape. Continue rolling remaining meat rolls and cabbage leaves. In the bottom of a lightly greased 12" x 11" x 2" roasting pan, spread chopped onions evenly. Arrange cabbage rolls in neat rows on top of the onions.

To Make Sauce: In a 2-quart saucepan, combine chili sauce and grape jelly with ¼ cup water, and heat over medium flame, stirring to melt jelly. Pour sauce over cabbage rolls. Cover the roasting pan tightly with foil. Bake in 350 degree oven for 2 hours. Remove foil, and brush rolls with sauce. Bake uncovered for 40 minutes more, or until sauce is thick and syrupy and cabbage rolls are glazed. Serve with sauce spooned over rolls.

Makes 28 cabbage rolls.

Cholent – from Wood-Burning Oven to Crockpot

"This recipe came from my grandmother, Rona, to my mother, Cecelia, and then to me. The only thing that changed was the method of cooking."   **Harriet Part**

I cup dried white beans (or baby lima beans), rinsed
3 pounds beef short ribs
Salt and pepper
I tablespoon oil
2 medium onions, thickly sliced
4 cloves garlic, minced
3 large carrots, cut into I-inch chunks
6 small White Rose potatoes, quartered
Salt, pepper and paprika
½ cup pearl barley, rinsed
2 cups beef stock

Soak beans for I hour in enough water to cover. Drain; set aside. Season meat lightly with salt and pepper. Heat a large skillet and add oil. Brown meat on each side in hot oil. Remove meat to a 3½-quart crockpot. In the same skillet, sauté onions, garlic, carrots and potatoes for 4 to 5 minutes over medium heat; season lightly with salt, pepper and paprika. Add vegetables, beans and barley to meat in crockpot. Pour in beef stock and stir gently. Cover and cook at 300 degrees for 8 hours.

Makes 4 to 6 servings.

Variation: This recipe can also be made in a large, 4-quart roasting pan and baked in 300 degree oven for 8 hours.

Chicken Fricassee for Rosh Hashanah

"My mom, Sherry, used to make this in a big yellow covered casserole pot. It was a labor of love!"
Marcia Goldenfeld Maiten

2 pounds ground beef or turkey, or mixture of both
1 extra large egg
⅓ cup soft bread crumbs
¼ cup grated onions
1–1½ teaspoons salt
Pepper to taste
¼ cup minced parsley
2 tablespoons oil (or more, if needed)
3 pounds boneless, skinless chicken breasts and thighs, cut into bite-sized pieces
6 chicken wings
½ pound chicken giblets (no liver)
Salt and pepper to taste
4 medium onions, finely chopped
2–3 cloves garlic, minced
1 cup finely chopped green or red pepper (optional)
2 cups chopped carrots
½ cup raisins or dried apricots
3–4 cups tomato sauce
1–2 cups chicken stock
½ cup minced parsley
1 tablespoon Worcestershire sauce
Salt to taste
Pepper to taste
Garlic, minced, to taste

In a large mixing bowl, combine ground beef or turkey with egg, bread crumbs, grated onion, salt, pepper and ¼ cup minced parsley. With wet hands, form mixture into small meatballs. Heat 2 tablespoons of oil in a large skillet, and sauté meatballs until browned on both sides and firm. Drain on paper towels and set aside. In the same skillet, add more oil if needed. Season chicken, giblets and wings with salt and pepper. Sauté in oil over medium heat until chicken is browned on all sides. Set aside. Add chopped onions and garlic to pan; cook until golden. Add peppers, carrots and raisins or apricots; cook for 5 minutes.

In a large Dutch oven or other large casserole, layer ingredients in this order until all are used: layer of vegetables and raisins (or apricots), layer of chicken pieces, layer of giblets and layer of meatballs. In a large measuring cup or bowl with pouring lip, combine tomato sauce, chicken stock, parsley, Worcestershire, salt, pepper and minced garlic to taste. Pour over ingredients in casserole. Cover and bake in 325 degree oven for 2 hours. Bake one day in advance. Cool and refrigerate. Next day, bring to room temperature, about 2 to 3 hours. Reheat, covered, in 325 degree oven for 1 hour before serving.

Makes 10 to 12 servings.

Honey Chicken with Tzimmes

"This dish has an old-time flavor usually associated with 'longtime cooking,' but this chicken is ready in just under 90 minutes." **Michael Turner**

1 cup pitted prunes
1 cup dried apricots
2½–3 pounds skinless chicken, cut up
1–2 yams (about 1 pound)
3 carrots, sliced
½ pound banana squash
Salt and pepper to taste
¾ teaspoon cinnamon
¼ teaspoon nutmeg
½ teaspoon ginger
1 cup honey

Soak prunes and apricots in warm water to cover for 30 minutes. Rinse chicken and place pieces in a greased 9" x 13" oven-tempered glass pan. Peel and slice vegetables; then add to chicken. Season with salt and pepper. Drain and add dried fruit. Combine cinnamon, nutmeg, ginger and honey; pour over chicken. Cover chicken with foil. Bake in 375 degree oven for 1 hour. Remove foil and bake for another 15 to 20 minutes, or until chicken is browned.

Makes 4 servings.

Barbecued Beef Brisket

"A recipe that's good any time of the year and pleases my family any time I make it!"   **Thelma Rifkind**

1 cup ketchup
1 cup water
1 tablespoon instant minced onion
2 tablespoons cider vinegar
1 tablespoon white horseradish
1 tablespoon prepared mustard
Salt to taste
$\frac{1}{2}$ teaspoon pepper
1 (4-pound) brisket
2 large onions, sliced
4–5 carrots, sliced into 2-inch chunks
5 medium potatoes, quartered

In a bowl, combine ketchup, water, instant onion, vinegar, horseradish, mustard, salt and pepper. Place brisket in a large, covered non-aluminum casserole dish, fat side up. Pour mixture over brisket. Marinate overnight.

Preheat oven to 350 degrees. Place onions on top of brisket and marinade. Cook, covered, for 2½ to 3 hours. Add carrots and potatoes. Continue cooking, covered, for 1 to 1½ hours more. Cool and refrigerate. Remove any accumulated fat from top. Slice meat, reheat and serve with vegetables, using pan juices as gravy.

Makes 8 servings.

Beef Short Ribs in a Crockpot

"It's the slow cooking that brings out the flavor!"   **Kate Golder Chapter**

1 (12-ounce) bottle chili sauce
½ cup dry red wine
½ cup chopped onions
1 clove garlic, minced
¼ cup light brown sugar
2 tablespoons wine vinegar
1 tablespoon prepared mustard
1 teaspoon seasoned salt
½ teaspoon seasoned pepper
3 pounds beef short ribs, trimmed of fat

In a large bowl, mix together the chili sauce, red wine, onions, garlic, sugar, vinegar, mustard, seasoned salt and pepper. Put about ½ cup in bottom of a 6-quart electric slow cooker. Dip each short rib in the remaining sauce and put in the cooker. Pour any remaining sauce over ribs. Cover and cook on the low heat setting for 10 to 11 hours.

Makes 4 to 6 servings.

Stuffed Breast of Veal with Two Stuffings

"I can still remember how good the noodle stuffing tasted." **Martha Goldberg,** *a resident at the Jewish Home*

Stuffed Breast of Veal

> 1 (4-5 pound) breast of veal trimmed of fat, with pocket for stuffing
> Salt, pepper, paprika and garlic to taste
> 1 cup coarsely chopped onions
> 1 cup coarsely chopped carrots
> 1 cup coarsely chopped celery
> 1½ cups beef stock

Potato Stuffing

> 2½ cups peeled, cubed potatoes
> 2 tablespoons olive oil
> 1 large onion, sliced into rings
> Salt and pepper to taste
> 1 egg

Noodle Stuffing

> 2 cups cooked, drained fine noodles
> 1 cup chopped onions
> ¼ cup finely chopped green pepper
> 1 tablespoon oil
> ½ teaspoon salt
> ¼ teaspoon each of garlic pepper and paprika, or more to taste

To Make Stuffed Breast of Veal: Season veal with salt, pepper, paprika and minced fresh garlic to taste. Stuff pocket with either Noodle Stuffing or Potato Stuffing. Use skewers to close pocket. Put veal in a 9" x 13" roasting pan along with onions, carrots and celery. Bake in 400 degree oven for 20 minutes. Spray meat with olive oil if veal looks dry.

Add 1½ cups beef stock to pan. Cover tightly with foil. Reduce heat to 350 degrees; continue baking for 2½ hours, basting frequently. Add more stock, if necessary. Let veal stand for 15 to 20 minutes before carving.

To Make Potato Stuffing: Cook potatoes until tender; drain and coarsely mash. In a skillet, heat 2 tablespoons olive oil; add onions and cook until well browned. Stir in potatoes plus salt and pepper to taste. Remove mixture from heat and stir in egg. Set aside until veal is ready to be stuffed.

To Make Noodle Stuffing: In a large bowl, combine noodles with onions and peppers that have been sautéed in oil until tender. Season with salt, garlic pepper and paprika. Add more to taste, if necessary. Stuff veal pocket as above.

Makes 4 to 5 servings.

Bubbe Feggie's Lukshen Kugel

"My bubbe Feggie was born in England. This recipe was hers and is at least three generations old. My mom gave me the recipe when I married." **Dorothy Salkin**

>   4 large eggs, separated
>   2 tablespoons unsalted butter
>   ¾ cup plus 2 tablespoon sugar
>   ½ cup nonfat milk
>   1 (12-ounce) package wide noodles, cooked and drained
>   ½ cup golden raisins
>   1½ pounds Granny Smith apples peeled, cored and thinly sliced
>   2½ teaspoons cinnamon
>   1 cup sliced almonds

In bowl of electric mixer, beat egg whites until they hold their shape but are not stiff. Set aside in another bowl. Using the same mixer bowl, beat butter, ¾ cup sugar and egg yolks until light and fluffy, about 3 minutes. Add milk and mix until well-combined. Remove bowl from mixer. Stir in cooked and cooled noodles and raisins. Fold egg whites into the noodle mixture.

Spray a 1½- or 2-quart round glass baking dish with butter-flavored spray. Arrange half of the apples in the bottom of the dish. Sprinkle with ½ teaspoon cinnamon. Spread half of noodle mixture over apples. Repeat with remaining apples, ½ teaspoon cinnamon and noodles. Place baking dish in center rack of oven and bake in 350 degree oven for 40 minutes. Combine remaining 2 tablespoons sugar, 1½ teaspoons cinnamon and nuts; sprinkle them on top of the kugel. Bake until top is golden and kugel is set, about 10 to 15 minutes.

Makes 6 servings.

Salmon with Egg-Lemon Sauce (Pescado Con Agristada)

"An early memory of holiday dinners was one that began with huge platters of fish prepared by my Aunt Mathilde Caraco. She was a native of Turkey and then the Isle of Rhodes." **Pearl Roseman**

Poached Fish

> 2½–3 cups water
> 1 teaspoon salt
> ½ teaspoon white pepper
> 1 carrot, cut into pieces
> 1 medium onion, cut into quarters
> ¼ cup chopped parsley
> 1½–2 pounds sliced salmon fillets, halibut or sole

Egg-Lemon Sauce

> 2 tablespoons margarine
> 2 tablespoons flour
> 2 cups stock (from above)
> 3 eggs, well beaten
> 4–5 tablespoons fresh lemon juice
> Salt and pepper to taste

To Make Fish: In a 9" x 13" x 3" roasting pan, put water, salt, pepper, carrots, onions and parsley. Bring to a simmer over low heat and cook for 20 minutes. Lay fish slices in the poaching liquid and continue to simmer for about 10 to 15 minutes, or until fish is easily flaked with a fork. Carefully remove fish to a serving platter; keep warm. Strain cooking liquid into a large measuring cup (should have 2 cups).

To Make Sauce: Melt margarine in a saucepan over medium heat. Whisk in flour until smooth and cook for a minute while stirring. Gradually whisk in the 2 cups of reserved stock and continue stirring until it comes to a boil. Turn heat lower. In a small bowl, beat eggs and lemon juice together. Slowly, add a little of the hot sauce to the egg mixture, mixing well; then stir mixture back into the pan. Whisk constantly until heated through, but do not boil. Season with salt and pepper to taste. Spoon over fish and serve.

Makes 4 to 6 servings.

Hint: A popular Greek restaurant adds artichoke hearts to this sauce – a nice addition.

Kasha Varnishkes
(Buckwheat and Bow-Tie Noodles)

Mollie Gornbein taught Valentine, a JHA cook, to make this recipe. Since the residents loved Mollie's recipe, now only Valentine is allowed to make the kasha.

2 large onions, finely chopped
4–6 tablespoons oil or chicken fat
1½ cups sliced mushrooms (optional)
1 (13-ounce) box kasha (roasted large-sized buckwheat)
1 teaspoon salt or garlic salt
½ teaspoon pepper or seasoned pepper
1 egg, beaten
2½–3 cups boiling beef stock, bouillon or water
½ (8-ounce) package bow-tie noodles, cooked and drained

In a large 12-inch skillet (with a tight-fitting lid), sauté onions in oil until browned. Add mushrooms, and sauté a few minutes longer. Stir in kasha, salt and pepper. Stir in beaten egg, and continue to stir until mixture looks dry. Add liquid slowly. Turn heat lower so that kasha will simmer. Cover and cook for about 10 minutes, or until liquid is absorbed. Stir in bow-tie pasta (varnishkes). Check for salt and pepper; if kasha is too dry, either add a little stock or a little oil.

Put kasha in casserole and cover tightly with lid or foil. Bake in 350 degree oven for 25 to 30 minutes, or until heated thoroughly. (Kasha can also be heated in microwave in a heatproof casserole, covered with plastic wrap. Cook on high for 3 to 4 minutes. Stir with a fork, cover again and heat for another 1 to 2 minutes or until fully heated).

Makes 8 to 10 servings.

Hint: Kasha may be made a day ahead and reheated; bring to room temperature and loosen with a fork.

Rita's Sweet-and-Sour Fish for 25

"I still make my mother's recipe for the sauce; she, however, uses a canned version – 'it's easier,' she says!"
Rita Wenger

Sweet-and-Sour Sauce

> 2 (6-ounce) cans tomato paste
> 1 quart plus ¼ cup water
> 10 cloves garlic, minced
> 2 cups finely chopped onions
> 2 medium green or red peppers, finely chopped
> 2 (15-ounce) cans pineapple tidbits
> 3 tablespoons minced parsley
> 1 tablespoon fresh dill
> ½–⅔ cup sugar
> 1 tablespoon salt, or more to taste
> 1 teaspoon pepper
> ½ cup fresh lemon juice

Fish

> 5 pounds (1½-inches thick) cod, cut into approximately 3-ounce pieces
> Flour
> 4 eggs, beaten
> ¼ cup water
> 1 teaspoon salt
> ½ teaspoon pepper
> 1 teaspoon paprika
> 1 cup flour
> Oil

To Make Sweet-and-Sour Sauce: In a 3-quart saucepan, put tomato paste and water; cook over moderate heat until mixture comes to a boil. Turn heat lower to simmer and add remaining ingredients. Simmer, uncovered, for 10 to 15 minutes. Taste for seasonings.

To Make Fish: Dredge fish pieces lightly with flour. Mix eggs with water, salt, pepper and paprika in a large shallow pan. Dip fish in egg mixture and then in flour. Heat oil, about 2 tablespoons, in a large griddle or skillet over moderate heat. Fry fish, about 4 to 5 pieces at a time, until lightly browned on both sides. Drain on paper towels and put fish side by side in two shallow 10" x 15" x 2" baking pans. Put 2–3 tablespoons Sweet-and-Sour Sauce over each piece of fish. Bake in 350 degree oven for 10 to 12 minutes, or until fish flakes easily when pierced with a fork.

Makes 25 servings.

Hint: This is a wonderful recipe to use for a sisterhood luncheon; recipe can easily be doubled.

Old-Fashioned Potato Latkes (Pancakes)

"These are popular all year-round but especially at Chanukah!"   **Claire Kunin**

4 large russet potatoes
1 small onion
1–1½ teaspoons salt
¼ teaspoon seasoned pepper
1 egg, beaten
3 tablespoons flour
Oil

Peel potatoes just before grating. Sprinkle with lemon juice and pat dry. Using a food processor with grater blade, grate potatoes and put in a colander to drain. Grate onion in fine grater or using steel blade. Mix in with potatoes. Using your hands, squeeze moisture from potato-onion mixture and put in a large mixing bowl. Stir in salt, pepper, beaten egg and flour.

Starting with 4 tablespoons of oil in a large skillet over moderate heat, wait until oil sizzles when a drop of potato mixture is put in pan. Drop potato mixture by the tablespoonful, spreading out to a circle with the back of the spoon. Fry until browned on both sides. Drain well on paper towels.

The pancakes can be served as an appetizer with dollops of sour cream and caviar or pieces of smoked salmon. They can also be made larger and served as a vegetable along with meat or poultry.

Makes 4 to 6 servings.

Hint: To re-crisp potato pancakes: Line cookie sheets with brown wrapping paper or bags (not recycled paper) to absorb oil; lay pancakes on paper and heat in 400 degree oven for 8 to 10 minutes or until hot.

Marinated Green Bean
and Red Pepper Salad

"This was a special favorite of my mother, Celia Kahn Aberman. It's a wonderful company dish because it is all prepared a day ahead." **Dorothy Salkin**

1 pound green beans
1 medium red pepper, seeded and cut into slivers
1 small red onion, thinly sliced and separated into rings
3 tablespoons red or white wine vinegar
1 tablespoon Dijon mustard
2 large cloves garlic, minced
½ teaspoon sugar
½ teaspoon dried basil
½ teaspoon salt
¼ teaspoon pepper
¼ cup safflower or olive oil
8 large lettuce leaves
Minced parsley
Crumbled feta cheese (optional)

Trim beans and cut each into two or three pieces. Pour water into a 3-quart saucepan to a depth of about 2 inches. Bring to a boil. Add green beans. Cook, uncovered, until just tender, about 5 minutes. Drain and rinse beans under cold water. Place in a shallow glass pan along with slivers of red pepper and red onion slices.

In a small mixing bowl, combine vinegar, mustard, garlic, sugar and basil; add salt and pepper to taste. Using a wire whisk, gradually beat in the oil until well blended. Spoon dressing over green beans, peppers and onions. Cover with plastic wrap or foil and refrigerate overnight until serving.

Put large lettuce leaves on a serving platter. Drain vegetables from dressing and place on lettuce leaves. Sprinkle with minced parsley (or crumbled feta cheese or both).

Makes 8 servings.

Lee Lee's Russian Tea Cakes

"This is my mother's recipe. There were always Russian tea cakes in the house when I was growing up. My mother saw to it that they were in her home and mine when my children were growing up. All my children's friends talk about raiding the freezer for Lee Lee's Russian tea cakes. My mom is gone now, but I have taken over making these cookies." **Marcia Schulman**

4 cups unsifted flour
3 teaspoons baking powder
½ teaspoon salt
¾ cup sugar
½ cup vegetable oil
½ cup melted margarine
¼ cup orange juice
1–2 teaspoons vanilla
3 eggs
Jelly (your favorite), stirred with a fork for easy spreading
1 cup raisins
Cinnamon-sugar mixture (1 teaspoon cinnamon and ½ cup sugar)
½ cup finely chopped walnuts or shredded coconut (optional)
1 egg white, slightly beaten

Sift flour, baking powder, salt and sugar together. Make a well in the center and add oil, margarine, juice, vanilla and eggs. Mix to form a soft dough. Knead 3 to 4 times on a lightly floured board, forming a smooth dough. Cut into 2 to 4 pieces and roll between 2 sheets of waxed paper to ¼-inch thickness. Spread with jelly and sprinkle with raisins, cinnamon-sugar mixture (saving 2 tablespoons for the topping), walnuts and coconut. Roll as you would a jelly roll. Brush with egg white. Sprinkle with remaining cinnamon-sugar mixture. Bake in preheated 350 degree oven for approximately 25 minutes. Cut into 1-inch-thick slices.

I Remember Mama

My Own Little Apple Cake

"This is the apple cake many remember their grandmas making. My grandmother (who was a resident at the Jewish Home) made it, and we still make it today!" **Annette Shapiro**

Cake

2 eggs, well beaten
1 cup vegetable oil
¾ cup sugar
Peel of 1 small lemon
2 cups flour
1 teaspoon baking powder
1½ teaspoons vanilla

Filling

4–5 medium Pippin apples, peeled and finely chopped
½ cup jam or ½ cup packed brown sugar
Juice of ½ lemon
2–3 teaspoons cinnamon
½ cup chopped walnuts (optional)
½ cup raisins (optional)
Sugar

To Make Cake: In bowl of electric mixer, beat eggs until foamy and add oil. With motor running on low, add sugar, lemon peel, flour, baking powder and vanilla, mixing well after each addition. Remove dough from mixer and form into a rectangle. Cut in half. Wrap dough in plastic wrap and refrigerate for 1 hour.

Roll out each half of the dough between 2 sheets of wax paper until each is about 9 inches square. Place 1 square in the bottom of a lightly greased 9-inch square baking pan. Place the other square on a cookie sheet. Refrigerate dough-lined pan and top crust until filling is prepared.

To Make Filling: In a medium bowl, combine apples, jam or sugar, lemon juice, cinnamon and nuts or raisins, and spread over dough in pan. Cover apples with remaining square of dough, pressing edges along inside of pan to seal; prick top with a fork. Sprinkle with a little sugar. Bake in preheated 350 degree oven for 1 hour or until top is golden brown. Cut into 9 squares after cake has cooled for at least 20 minutes.

A Very Special Sponge Cake

"So moist with a wonderful citrus flavor, this cake is good plain or used as a base for mousse cakes or fruit-filled shortcakes. My mother, Claire Summers-Center, used to let this cake cool upside down on a milk bottle!"
Anita Tamar

> 8 large eggs, separated
> 1 cup sugar
> 1½ cups cake flour, sifted then measured
> 3 tablespoons orange juice
> 5 tablespoons fresh lemon juice
> ¼ teaspoon grated lemon peel
> ¼ teaspoon salt
> ½ cup sugar

In bowl of electric mixer, beat egg yolks until thick, about 4 to 5 minutes. Continue beating, gradually adding sugar. Set mixer on low speed; add flour, juices and peel alternately.

In a separate bowl, beat egg whites and salt on low speed. While beating slowly, wait until soft peaks form before gradually adding ½ cup sugar, 1 tablespoon at a time. Beat just until stiff. Do not overbeat.

Fold meringue carefully into the flour mixture by first adding a big dollop of meringue to lighten batter. Then, fold in remaining meringue. Using a rubber spatula, carefully put mixture into an ungreased 10-inch tube pan. Bake in preheated 325 degree oven for 55 to 60 minutes or until cake starts to pull away from sides. Cool cake upside down over bottle.

Makes 12 to 16 servings.

Old-Fashioned Buttermilk Chocolate Cake

"I have been making this cake for 42 years and the lady who gave it to me said it was 100 years old then. It still is the best chocolate cake I have ever tasted."　**Harriet Part**

Cake

> 2 cups sugar
> ½ cup (1 stick) butter or margarine
> 2 eggs
> 1 teaspoon vanilla
> 3 squares unsweetened chocolate, melted
> ½ cup buttermilk
> 2 cups flour
> 2 teaspoons baking soda
> 1 teaspoon salt
> 1 cup boiling water

Chocolate Glaze

> ¼ cup (½ stick) butter
> 1 tablespoon cognac or other liqueur
> 2 tablespoons water
> 3 tablespoons white corn syrup
> Dash salt
> 4 ounces semisweet chocolate chips

To Make Cake: In bowl of electric mixer, cream sugar and butter until well blended. Add eggs, vanilla and melted chocolate; continue beating until smooth. Add buttermilk and flour (that has been combined with soda and salt) alternately to chocolate mixture, blending after each addition. Add boiling water and mix until smooth (batter is thin).

Pour batter into greased and floured 10-inch baking pan or two 9-inch baking pans. Bake in preheated 350 degree oven for 45 minutes for 10-inch pan and 35 minutes for 9-inch pans. Cool in pan for 10 minutes before removing. Cool completely and refrigerate or freeze. Frost an hour before serving.

To Make Chocolate Glaze: In a medium-sized saucepan, bring butter, cognac, water, syrup and salt to a boil. Remove from heat. Add chocolate; cover saucepan and let stand for 5 minutes; stir until well blended. Cool until glaze thickens to consistency of whipping cream. Pour all of the glaze onto the middle of the cake and spread over top and sides with a spatula.

Hint: Can substitute buttermilk by combining ½ cup milk and 1½ teaspoons white vinegar.

Walnut Wave Pistachio Bundt Cake

"This is one of the best 'easy cakes' you'll ever make. It was my mother's recipe and the family loved it."
Susan Bobrow

> 1 (18-ounce) package yellow cake mix
> 1 (3.4-ounce) package pistachio instant pudding
> 4 eggs
> 1 cup sour cream
> ½ cup vegetable oil
> ½ cup sugar
> 1 teaspoon cinnamon
> 1 cup chopped walnuts or pistachios

Beat cake mix, pudding, eggs, sour cream and oil together until well blended. Mix sugar, cinnamon and nuts in a separate bowl. Pour half the batter into a greased and floured 12-cup bundt pan. Sprinkle with half of the sugar-nut mixture. Pour in rest of batter. Sprinkle with rest of sugar-nut mixture. Bake in preheated 350 degree oven for about 50 minutes or until toothpick inserted in cake comes out clean.

Makes 12 servings.

Lazy Daisy Cake

"My mom, Eva Bass, used to make this cake for big gatherings. The flavor is wonderful, and it's easy to make."
Bobbi Delevie

Cake

> 4 eggs
> 2 cups sugar
> 2 teaspoons vanilla
> 2 scant cups cake flour
> 1 tablespoon baking powder
> 1/2 teaspoon salt
> 1 cup milk
> 4 tablespoons butter

Frosting

> 1 cup brown sugar, packed
> 1/3 cup heavy cream
> 1/2 cup melted butter
> 1 1/2 cups coconut

To Make Cake: Combine eggs, sugar and vanilla in bowl of electric mixer. Beat until thick. Combine flour, baking powder and salt; slowly add to egg mixture, beating until well blended. Heat milk and butter to boiling point and slowly add to batter. Beat just until well combined. Pour mixture into buttered 9 1/2" x 13" cake pan and bake 25 to 30 minutes in preheated 350 degree oven until top springs back when touched. Remove cake from oven and frost immediately; return cake to 450 degree oven or slip under broiler just until top turns a golden brown. Serve warm or at room temperature.

To Make Frosting: While cake is baking, combine brown sugar, cream, melted butter and coconut.

Makes 12 to 16 servings.

English Spice Cake

This unusually made cake came to us via Canada and Palm Springs. A "snow-bird" by the name of Etta Goldman brought it to the Jewish Home.

Cake

1 cup oil
2 cups cold water
¾ cups sugar
¾ cup brown sugar, packed
½ teaspoon ground cloves
2 teaspoons cinnamon
1 cup raisins (golden or dark)
4 cups flour
2 teaspoons baking soda
½ teaspoon baking powder
1 cup chopped walnuts

Lemon Glaze

6 tablespoons fresh lemon juice
2 teaspoons grated lemon peel
½ teaspoon lemon flavoring
1½ cups sifted powdered sugar

To Make Cake: In a 2-quart saucepan, combine oil, water, both sugars, cloves, cinnamon and raisins; bring to a boil, stirring occasionally. Turn heat off and cool to room temperature. In a bowl, combine flour, baking soda and baking powder. Stir liquid into flour mixture. Add walnuts, and stir batter until ingredients are well blended.

Pour batter into a well-greased and slightly floured 9" x 13" baking pan. Bake in preheated 350 degree oven for 45 minutes or until a toothpick comes out clean. Cool in pan for 10 minutes. Spoon glaze over warm cake; then cool before serving.

To Make Lemon Glaze: In a small bowl, mix fresh lemon juice, lemon peel, lemon flavoring and sugar.

Makes 12 to 16 servings.

Holiday Date and Nut Cake

"This was one of the first recipes my mother taught me. I can still taste how yummy it was with a big spoonful of whipped cream." **Fran Stengel**

 1 teaspoon baking soda
 1¼ cups boiling water
 1½ cups dates, chopped
 1 tablespoon butter or margarine, melted
 1¼ cups sugar
 1 egg
 1 teaspoon vanilla
 ¼ teaspoon salt
 1¼ cups flour, sifted
 ¾ cup chopped nuts

Dissolve baking soda in water and pour over dates in a mixing bowl. Let stand until cool. Cream butter or margarine and sugar in bowl of electric mixer. Add egg, vanilla and salt. Combine with dates. Add flour and nuts. Spread batter in a greased 7½" x 12" baking pan. Bake in preheated 300 degree oven for 50 to 60 minutes until very brown. Serve with whipped cream, if desired.

Almond Strudel

"My great-aunt Ida, who was from Turkey, made the most unusual and delicious strudel, which she brought to every wedding and Bar Mitzvah. She would never share the recipe, but I will!" **Harriet Part**

> 2 cups blanched almonds
> 1½ cups powdered sugar
> 1 extra-large egg white, slightly beaten, or 2 tablespoons corn syrup
> 1 tablespoon fresh lemon juice
> ¼ teaspoon almond extract
> 8 large sheets fillo (phyllo) dough (from 1-pound package)
> Butter-flavored non-stick cooking spray (or 1 stick unsalted butter, melted)
> 1 cup vanilla cookie crumbs

In a blender or food processor, whirl almonds until fine. In bowl of electric mixer, thoroughly blend almonds with powdered sugar, egg white, lemon juice and almond extract.

Using 8 sheets of fillo dough from a refrigerated package, lay the sheets on a dry surface. (Picture an open book.) Fold the fillo sheets in half. Working from the bottom up, spray each half sheet with non-stick spray and a light sprinkling of fine cookie crumbs. Repeat the process with the other half of fillo sheets. Spray the top sheet with cooking spray and sprinkle lightly with cookie crumbs. (The book is now completely open.)

Mold the almond mixture with your hands into a long roll, about the length of the fillo sheets. Place almond roll at one end of fillo sheet. Fold in sides (edges) and roll like a jelly roll. Brush or spray seam and press to close. Lift carefully and place roll, seam side down, on a greased cookie sheet, using spray or brushing with melted butter. Cut slits through top of strudel only, 1½ inches apart (serving size). Bake in 375 degree oven for 20 to 30 minutes. Remove from oven and let cool on baking sheet. Sprinkle with powdered sugar after strudel is cut into pieces. Strudel may be kept frozen.

Makes 10 to 12 servings.

Granny's Famous (and Secret) Mandelbread

"When I first learned that my grandmother, Betty Goldberg, was going blind, I asked her to make her secret mandelbread. I watched and wrote down the recipe as no one in the family knew how to make it. For the most part, this is how grandma told it to me. And as grandma would say, 'Be sure to hum just any tune as you go.'"
Stacy Becker

> **3 eggs at room temperature (4 if they are small)**
> **1 cup sugar**
> **¾ cup vegetable oil**
> **Juice of 1 fresh orange**
> **4–5 shakes cinnamon**
> **2 caps vanilla (use the cap of the vanilla bottle)**
> **1 teaspoon baking soda (these are regular spoons)**
> **2 teaspoons baking powder**
> **3½–4 cups flour**
> **2½ tablespoons poppy seeds**
> **1 cup blanched slivered almonds**
> **Cinnamon-sugar (1 tablespoon sugar and ½ teaspoon cinnamon)**

Use mixer to whip eggs and sugar. Add oil, orange juice, cinnamon and vanilla. Meanwhile, mix baking soda and powder with flour. Add flour mixture into wet mixture gradually, mixing constantly. Dough will get thick "like cement." (It is better for the dough to be too thick rather than too thin.) Turn off the mixer; add poppy seeds and nuts.

Use the oil that has now settled at the bottom of your measuring cup by dripping it on a large cookie sheet with sides. Spray the sheet as well. ("This recipe is exact and authentic.") Your goal is to make 4 wide strips of dough across the pan (the short width of the pan). Leave about 1½ inches of room between the rows to avoid the strips spreading into each other. Sprinkle top of dough with cinnamon-sugar mixture.

Bake in preheated 350 degree oven for approximately 35 to 40 minutes. Use a serrated knife to cut the four rows apart if they run together and to cut each row into thin strips. (However, if bread is crumbly, bake longer before cutting.) Separate slices to allow for further drying. Return to oven for 10 minutes at the same temperature. Turn cookies over for further drying; return to 275 degree oven for 15 minutes. Cool and serve.

Hamantaschen

"This is a wonderful dough to work with. My grandmother, Julia Gast Wollman, used this dough for hamantaschen, and now it's a tradition in our family." **Deena Gordon**

Hamantaschen

> 3 eggs
> ¾ cup oil
> ¼ cup orange juice
> ⅓ cup water
> 1 teaspoon vanilla
> 3 cups flour, sifted
> 1 cup sugar
> 3 teaspoons baking powder
> 2 cups flour

Filling

> 1 (17-ounce) jar lekvar (prune butter) or 1 (12-ounce) can poppyseed filling
> 2 teaspoons orange juice

To Make Hamantaschen: Combine eggs, oil, juice, water and vanilla in a large mixing bowl. Combine and add dry ingredients, except for 2 cups flour, to the liquid mixture. Let stand for ½ hour. Make a well with 2 cups of flour and pour mixture into well. Mix with a fork to combine; then knead lightly until dough holds together.

Roll out dough on a lightly floured surface. Cut into circles, using a 3-inch cookie cutter. Place ½ teaspoon of filling into center of circle. Pinch dough together in three places to form a tri-cornered hat. Place hamantaschen onto a well-greased cookie sheet and bake in preheated 350 degree oven for 12 to 15 minutes or until golden brown. Repeat process until all the dough is used.

To Make Filling: Combine lekvar or poppyseed filling with orange juice. May substitute prune filling or poppyseed filling with apricot, apple or cherry jam.

Makes 50 to 60 small hamantaschen.

Poppyseed Cookies

"Of all the poppyseed cookies that I've baked, this one reminds everyone of their family's old-time favorite."
Zelda White

3 cups flour
1 cup sugar
¾ cup oil
3 eggs
½ teaspoon salt
1 teaspoon baking powder
Grated peel of 1 orange
2–3 tablespoons poppy seeds
2 tablespoons sugar

In bowl of electric mixer, combine flour, sugar, oil, eggs, salt, baking powder, orange peel and poppy seeds until ingredients are mixed well. Lightly flour surface of work area. Divide dough into 4 sections. Roll out 1 section at a time to about ⅓ inch thick. Use a 3-inch cookie cutter to make cookies. Sprinkle with sugar. Bake in preheated 350 degree oven until edges of cookies are lightly browned, about 20 to 30 minutes. Bake longer for crunchier cookies.

Makes 24 to 30 cookies.

Apricot Walnut Rugelach

"This was Aunt Rose's claim to fame in a family of great bakers – no one else dared to make it."
Harriet Part

> 2 sticks butter (1 cup), sliced into pieces
> 1 (8-ounce) package regular or light cream cheese, cut into 6 pieces
> ¾ cup sugar
> 3 cups flour
> Apricot or raspberry jam
> 1 cup finely chopped walnuts
> 1 teaspoon cinnamon
> 4 tablespoons sugar
> Milk

In bowl of food processor using steel blade, put butter, cream cheese and ¾ cup sugar. Turn motor on and off until mixture is well blended. Distribute flour evenly around bowl and turn motor on until dough starts to form and come together. Remove blade from machine. Take out dough and form into a large, flat rectangle. Cut dough into 4 pieces. Reshape each piece into a flat round disc. Wrap each disc in wax paper and refrigerate for at least 2 hours or overnight. Dough can also be frozen. Remove 1 disc at a time to roll out.

On a lightly floured board or marble top, roll out dough into a circle about ⅛ inch thick. Loosen underneath dough with a long spatula. Beat jam with fork (start with ½ cup and add if needed), and spread a thin layer evenly over circle, stopping ½ inch from the border. In a small bowl, mix walnuts, cinnamon and sugar; sprinkle ¼ of cinnamon mixture over layer of jam. With a sharp knife, cut circle in half, then in quarters and each quarter into 3 triangles. Roll each triangle from wide end to point. Curve into crescent shape.

Put rugelach on a foil-lined cookie sheet, about 2 inches apart. Brush rugelach with milk and sprinkle with any remaining cinnamon mixture. Press in slightly. Bake in preheated 375 degree oven until lightly browned, about 15 to 18 minutes. Cool on rack before storing.

Makes approximately 48 small rugelach.

Old-Fashioned Coffee Jelly

"A simple but elegant party dessert! This was popular years ago and is popular once again."   **Zelda White**

> 1 tablespoon gelatin
> ¼ cup coffee-flavored liqueur
> 1½ cups hot strong coffee
> ⅓ cup sugar
> Whipped cream
> Cinnamon or shaved chocolate

In a small bowl, soften gelatin in liqueur for 10 minutes. Gradually stir in hot strong coffee and sugar. Stir mixture until gelatin is completely dissolved. Pour mixture into 4 glass dessert dishes. Chill until set. Garnish with lightly sweetened whipped cream, a sprinkling of cinnamon or shaved chocolate.

Makes 4 servings.

Hint: You can also mold this dessert in small coffee cups.

Brown Sugar Brownies

"This was my mother's recipe. It's easy to make and popular with everyone who tries it."
Madeline R. Goodwin

> 1 stick butter or margarine
> 2 squares bittersweet chocolate, broken into pieces
> 2 cups brown sugar, packed
> 2 eggs
> 1 teaspoon vanilla
> 1 cup flour
> 1 cup ground walnuts or pecans

Melt butter in a saucepan over low heat. Pour just enough of the melted butter to evenly coat bottom of a 9" x 9" square pan. Put pieces of chocolate in the saucepan and return to low heat. Stir in brown sugar, eggs and vanilla until sugar has melted. Remove from heat and stir in flour and then nuts. Pour into the prepared pan. Bake in 350 degree oven for 30 minutes or until toothpick inserted into center comes out clean. Cool for 20 minutes. Loosen edges. Cut into squares. When ready to serve brownies, sift powdered sugar over tops.

Makes 16 squares.

Sesame Ring Cookies (Biscochos)

"These cookies are crunchy and a longtime Sephardic favorite."   **Anita Tamar**

4 large eggs
1 cup sugar
½ cup vegetable oil
4½ cups flour
4 teaspoons baking powder
1 teaspoon salt
1 tablespoon sugar
1 cup sesame seeds

In bowl of electric mixer, beat eggs until well blended. Reserve 4 tablespoons of egg and set aside. Beat in sugar and add oil; continue beating for 1 minute. Combine flour, baking powder and salt. Gradually add flour mixture to egg mixture to make a smooth dough.

Use floured hands to shape dough into ropes, about ½ inch in diameter. Cut ropes into 4½-inch-long pieces. Pinch ends together to form a ring. Place rings on greased cookie sheets.

Mix 1 tablespoon sugar with reserved egg. Brush tops of rings with egg wash. Sprinkle rings heavily with sesame seeds. Bake in preheated 350 degree oven for 15 to 20 minutes or until golden brown. Remove from sheets and cool on wire racks.

Makes 3 dozen rings.

Company Peach Cobbler

"A sophisticated combination of flavors in a down-home dessert that's luscious."   **Thelma Rifkind**

10 large, firm ripe peaches (4½ pounds)
1½ cups sugar
3 tablespoons cornstarch
⅓ cup orange juice
2 teaspoons vanilla
2 cups flour
½ cup finely chopped crystallized ginger
1 tablespoon baking powder
1 cup heavy cream
4 tablespoons butter, melted
Vanilla ice cream (optional)

Peel, pit and thickly slice peaches into a large bowl. Combine ½ cup sugar with the cornstarch; sprinkle over peaches. Gently stir to evenly coat the slices. Add orange juice and vanilla; stir gently. Spoon into a buttered 3- to 3½-quart baking dish (about 9" x 13"). Set aside.

In a large bowl, combine flour, ginger, 2 tablespoons of remaining sugar and baking powder. Stirring with a fork, slowly add cream until mixture is just combined and batter resembles cookie dough. Scoop about ⅓ cup batter into a 2-inch ball. Flatten, dip both sides of the ball in melted butter and then in remaining sugar. Place on top of fruit. Repeat and make about 8 flattened balls. Place balls 1 inch apart over fruit. Bake in preheated 350 degree oven for 1 hour or until center bubbles and top is golden brown. Do not overcook – it will dry out! Let cobbler cool at least 15 minutes. Serve with ice cream, if desired.

Makes 8 servings.

Mom's "All-American" Apple Pie

"My mother, Annette Bozman, loved to bake apple pies. Her advice was to be sure to use fresh lemon juice sprinkled over the apples to bring out the apple flavor."   **B. Bozman**

Crust

> 2 cups flour
> 1 teaspoon salt
> ½ cup vegetable oil
> ¼ cup cold water

Filling

> 2–2½ pounds pippin or Granny Smith apples
> 2–3 teaspoons fresh lemon juice
> ¾–1 cup sugar, or more if apples are tart
> 1 teaspoon cinnamon
> ¼ teaspoon nutmeg

To Make Crust: In a large mixing bowl, combine flour and salt. Pour oil and then cold water into a measuring cup, but do not mix together. Pour oil and water all at the same time into the flour. Stir with a fork until crumbly and dough looks moist. Press dough into a smooth ball. Cut in half and flatten slightly. Refrigerate for 20 minutes. Work with 1 piece of dough at a time.

With a damp sponge or dishcloth, dampen counter top or marble top. Put a 12-inch square of wax paper on damp area and smooth out. Put ½ of the dough on top of paper. Place another 12-inch piece of wax paper on top of dough. Roll from the center out to different directions to ⅛-inch-thick round. Peel off top paper. Lift and place carefully over 9-inch pie plate. Peel off paper. Gently fit pastry into pan. Refrigerate while preparing filling.

To Make Filling: Peel apples; quarter; remove cores and slice them into a large mixing bowl. Sprinkle with lemon juice and toss together. Mix in sugar, cinnamon and nutmeg. Mound apples in bottom crust. Roll out top crust as described above. Place over apples. Press bottom and top crust together and seal by pressing edges with a fork (or fluting). Cut 3 or 4 small ½-inch slits around center of pie to let steam escape. Bake in preheated 425 degree oven for 40 to 45 minutes. If crust gets too brown, cover with foil.

Hint: If apples seem very juicy while preparing filling, add 2 tablespoons flour to the sugar.

I Remember Mama

Recipe Contributors

The Cookbook committee expresses its deep appreciation to the residents and friends of the Jewish Home for the Aging who contributed their recipes. We regret that many recipes could not be included due to similarity or lack of space. Additionally, some recipes were revised to meet the requirements of the cookbook.

Marcia Abelson
Celia Kahn Aberman
Brenda Abramson
Florence Altura
Sylvia Aptekar
Shirley Arenson[R]
Robin Armstrong
Phil Arneson
Don Arthur
Elayne Barco
Betty Barocas
Sandy Baron
Eva Bass*
Charlotte Beck
Stacy Becker
Pauline Bender
Sarita Benzadon
Ricki Bergman
Libbie Berman[R]
Rita Berman
Barbara Bernstein
Florence Bernstein
Dodo Bienenfeld
Betty Binder
Lisa Birch
Lynn Blatt
Miriam Bloom
Jan Blumenthal
Susan Bobrow
Helen Bolker*
Rose Bornstein
Bess Boroditsky[R]
Judy Bort
Annette Bozman[R]
Barbara Bozman
Sara Braver
Elaine Burakoff
Renée Lang Burg
Claire Summers Center*

Minnie Chapman*
Laura Chick, Los Angeles City
  Councilmember
Natalie Clapick
Gayle Cohen
Jennie Cohen
Katherine Cohen
Rica Cohen
Robin Cohen
Syra Cohn[R]
Rae Cooper
Dagne Crane
Nanette Cutler
Lauren J. Dale
Vicki Davis
Velma Dean
Celia de Lavallade[R]
Bobbi Delevie
Lorraine Dennis
Tova Dershowitz
Ilse Diament
Shelley Diament
Sheila Dick
Dena Dorfman
Helen Dorn
Arlene Dunn
Gloria Esses
Ada Fallick
Sandy Firestone
Harriett Fishbein
Judy Fishman
Nancy Fox
Frances Franco
Rhea Frantz
Carole Friedman
Bobbie Fromberg
Rayna Gabin
Caryl Geiger
Estelle Gershowitz

Dinah Gerson
Gloria Getzug
Ruth Gilliam
Lee Glanzer[R]
Edith Glasser
Betty Goldberg
Jacqueline Goldberg
Martha Goldberg[R]
Mali Goldenberg
Sarah Goldenberg
Sherry Goldenfeld*
Members of the
  Kate Golder Chapter
Etta Goldman[R]
Annabel Goldstein
Anne Goldstein
Lillian Goldstein
Stacey Goldstein
Bella Goldstine
Roz Goldstine
Madeline Goodwin
Rabbi Bill Gordon
Deena Gordon
Mollie Gornbein[R]
Lisa Gottlieb
Pattikay Gottlieb
Robin Gottlieb
Daryl Gradinger
Marilyn Grass
Bettie Gray
Debbie Green
Randi Green
Suzanne Greenberg
Alice Greenfield
Shelley Greenspan[R]
Renay Gregg
Catherine Halfon
Liz Harris
Shirley Hart

Sybel Heller
Jackie Hirtz
Edythe Hock
Betty Jackson
Fern Jubas
Sybil Kaplan
Miriam Kasman
Marcia Katz
Ann Kaufman
Ginny Kikta
Ruth Kleifeld
Barbara Klein
Sandi Knoff
Ella Kohn
Claire Kunin
Juell Laub[R]*
Tracy Lee
Anne Leff
Sandra Leib
Sandy Leiman
Betty Lenchner
Barbara Lenox
Marty Leskin
Cecelia Lesser*
Judith Leventhal
Barbara Levy
Allyne Lewis
Linda Linden
Dorothy Lipcowitz[R]
Joan Lippman
Evy Lutin
Marcia Goldenfeld Maiten
Mickey Mandell
Lee Margolin
Annette Marks
Betty Martin
Miriam Mason
Marilyn Mathews
Linda Matloff
Bobbi McRae
Anna Medvin[R]
Rick Mendosa
Rona Miesels*
Jan Miller
Edna Mily*
Sandy Mindlin
Sandy Mittleman

Rhoda Monkarsh
Beverly Morhaime
Jeff Nelken
Grace Nevell
Britta Noonan
Ruth Nussbaum
Fran Oppenheimer
September Orlando
Helen Ouslander
Sylvia Ovitz
Harriet Part
Shana Passman
Al Passy
Annette Peters
Elaine Pfefferman
Marsha Pink
Susan Pleskus
Rose Poler
Rabbi Deborah Prinz
Sadye Pucker[R]
Eileen Puelicher
Susan Raphael
Gail Ravins
Roslyn Ravitz
Jess Rifkind
Thelma Rifkind
Pearl Roseman
Pearl Rosen[R]
Ida Rosenbaum
Lillian Ross[R]
Sam Rothman[R]
Leslie Rouff
Carol Rowen
Dorothy Salkin
Beverly Saperstein
Sylvia Saxon
Reggie Scheer
Barbara Scheinman
Jilliene Schenkel
Kelly Schiffer
Ruth Schneider[R]
Steve Schoneberg
Marcia Schulman
Deborah Schwartz
Mildred Schwartz[R]
Carol Scott
Phyllis Scott

Blanche Segal*
Esther Shadrow
Annette Shapiro
Brad Sherman
Annejo Shirring
Joya Shore
Janice Shulman
Micki Siegel
Michelle Simon
Dora Sitkin
Iris Smotrich
Betty Sonnett
Joan Specter
Sarah Spielman[R]
Linda Spitz
Betty Steiner
Fran Stengel
Robin Stotter
DeeDee Sussman
Gail Sussman
Cecile Talsky
Anita Tamar
Rehovit Tanner
Edith Taylor
Leigh Tepper
Lillian Topin
Sarah Treves
Michael Turner
Ronna Wallace
Sherry Watnick
Belle Weis
Reneé Weitzer
Fritzie Welan
Tova Weltman
Rita Wenger
Zelda White
Sam Wigoda
Sue Wolf
Monica Wolfe
Bernice Wolin
Julia Wollman*
Shirley Yudis
Simone Zelden
Carol Zuckerman
Dee Zuckerman

* In Blessed Memory
[R] Jewish Home for the Aging Resident

Glossary

Ashkenazi	Jews of Middle or Eastern European descent.
Baba Ghanoosh	A popular Mediterranean eggplant dish.
Biscochos	Any crunchy cookie. See *Mandelbread*.
Blintzes	Crêpes filled with cheese or fruit.
Borekas	Middle Eastern meat, cheese or spinach-filled turnovers.
Borscht	Hot or cold beet, cabbage or spinach soup.
Challah	Braided egg bread usually served on the Sabbath and holidays. Sometimes made circular with raisins.
Chanukah	Festival of Lights. Latkes are traditionally served.
Cholent	A stove-top stew made with meat, vegetables and beans cooked for eight to twelve hours.
Dolma	Rolled stuffed vegetable.
Farfel	Crumbled pieces of matzos.
Gefilte Fish	Poached fish balls usually made from ground carp, whitefish or pike mixed with eggs, salt, onions and pepper.
Haroset (Charoset)	A mixture of chopped apples, nuts, cinnamon and wine symbolizing the mortar used by the Jews building Egyptian pyramids. Served at Passover.
Kasha	Buckwheat groats.
Kasha Varnishkes	Seasoned buckwheat groats combined with bow-tie noodles.
Knaidlach	See *Matzo Balls*.

Knishes	Little flaky pastries filled with meat, potatoes and onions.
Kreplach	A triangular or square-shaped dumpling filled with meat, cheese or vegetables.
Kugel	A casserole or pudding made of noodles or potatoes.
Latkes	Pancakes usually made with potatoes but can be made with other vegetables.
Lox	Smoked salmon.
Mandelbread	A twice-baked cookie, also called *"biscochos"* by the Sephardic community.
Matzo Balls	Made with matzo meal, eggs and sometimes chicken fat. Cooked with chicken soup.
Passover (Pesach)	Celebrates the liberation of Jews from Egypt. For eight days, only unleavened foods are eaten.
Rosh Hashanah	The Jewish New Year. Marks the beginning of the Jewish High Holidays.
Sephardic	Jews descended from those who once lived in Spain.
Shabbat	The Jewish Sabbath, which starts at sundown Friday and ends at sundown Saturday.
Strudel	Filled pastry made from thin flaky dough.
Sukkot	The harvest festival of thanksgiving.
Tahini	Made from ground sesame seeds and used in preparing hummus.
Tzimmes	A dish made with prunes, carrots, yams and sweet potatoes. Can also be prepared with meat. This dish is served on Rosh Hashanah to celebrate a sweet New Year.
Yom Kippur	High Holy Day. Day of Atonement. Requires 24 hours of fasting. The Break-the-Fast meal is served at the end of Yom Kippur.

Index